Making Heritage Together

T0383585

Making Heritage Together presents a case study of public archaeology by focusing on the collaborative creation of knowledge about the past with a rural community in central Crete. It is based on a long-term archaeological ethnography project that engaged this village community in collectively researching, preserving and managing their cultural heritage.

This volume presents the theoretical and local contexts for the project, explains the methodology and the project outcomes, and reviews in detail some of the public archaeology actions with the community as examples of collaborative, research-based heritage management. What the authors emphasize in this book is the value of local context in designing and implementing public archaeology projects, and the necessity of establishing methods to understand, collaborate and interact with culturally specific groups and publics. They argue for the implementation of archaeological ethnographic research as a method of creating instances and spaces for collaborative knowledge production. The volume contributes to a greater understanding of how rural communities can be successfully engaged in the management of their own heritage.

It will be relevant to archaeologists and other heritage professionals who aim to maximize the inclusivity and impact of small projects with minimal resources and achieve sustainable processes of collaboration with local stakeholders.

Aris Anagnostopoulos is an anthropologist, historian and writer. His research focuses on the poetics and politics of the past. He currently works as a public programs director with the HERITAGE and holds an honorary lectureship at the University of Kent.

Evangelos 'Vanghelis' Kyriakidis is the founding director of the Heritage Management Organization (HERITAGE) and the director of the Three Peak Sanctuaries project (Kent-HERITAGE). He focuses on heritage management, prehistoric archaeology and Mycenaean administration.

Eleni Stefanou is an archaeologist and museologist, working for Hellenic Open University and HERITAGE. Her research focuses on the politics of the past. She has been teaching museum studies, museum education and cultural heritage management at Greek Universities since 2008.

Making Heritage Together

Archaeological Ethnography
and Community Engagement
with a Rural Community

**Aris Anagnostopoulos, Evangelos
Kyriakidis and Eleni Stefanou**

LONDON AND NEW YORK

First published 2022
by Routledge
4 Park Square, Milton Park, Abingdon, Oxon OX14 4RN

and by Routledge
605 Third Avenue, New York, NY 10158

*Routledge is an imprint of the Taylor & Francis Group, an
informa business*

British Library Cataloguing-in-Publication Data
A catalogue record for this book is available from the British Library

Library of Congress Cataloging-in-Publication Data
Names: Anagnostopoulos, Aris, author. | Kyriakidis, Evangelos,
    author. | Stefanou, Eleni, author.
Title: Making heritage together: archaeological ethnography
    and community engagement with a rural community/Aris
    Anagnostopoulos, Evangelos Kyriakidis, Eleni Stefanou.
Other titles: Archaeological ethnography and community engagement
    with a rural community
Description: Abingdon, Oxon; New York: Routledge, 2022. |
    Includes bibliographical references and index.
Identifiers: LCCN 2021058841 (print) | LCCN 2021058842 (ebook) |
    ISBN 9781032194745 (hardback) | ISBN 9781032194769 (paperback) |
    ISBN 9781003259367 (ebook)
Subjects: LCSH: Archaeology and state—Greece—Crete—Case
    studies. | Goniés (Greece)—Antiquities. | Three Peak Sanctuaries of
    Central Crete Project—History.
Classification: LCC DF261.C8 A53 2022 (print) | LCC DF261.C8 (ebook) |
    DDC 949.5/9—dc23/eng/20220112
LC record available at https://lccn.loc.gov/2021058841
LC ebook record available at https://lccn.loc.gov/2021058842

ISBN: 978-1-032-19474-5 (hbk)
ISBN: 978-1-032-19476-9 (pbk)
ISBN: 978-1-003-25936-7 (ebk)

DOI: 10.4324/9781003259367

Typeset in Times New Roman
by KnowledgeWorks Global Ltd.

To the memory of Christos Panteris

Contents

Figures

Preface and acknowledgments

This is a book that straddles many disciplines, has multiple aims and may be said to have been written by a multiplicity of authors. First and foremost, it aims to document the collaborative work on archaeology and heritage done in a village in the Cretan mountains by archaeologists, anthropologists, museologists, artists and local inhabitants. This project, the *Three Peak Sanctuaries of Central Crete* project, began as an archaeological project without emphasis on any single village community. Yet, it soon invested most of its time and energy in a community engagement project with the population of the village of Gonies, who actively sought to direct its methodological considerations toward areas that were more interesting to the village itself. The ethnographic aspect of the project, initially geared toward enriching archaeological accounts and investigating the relationship between local identity and the archaeological past, acquired a more encompassing character, as a space for encounter of different publics, groups, persons and outlooks. Given the character of the village, and its historical trajectory, especially in view of its recent depopulation in the latter half of the twentieth century, this project became much more than research on the archaeological landscape of a rural community in Crete. It also became a study in the uses, methods and ultimate goals of community engagement with a resilient group of mostly elderly people. This transformation, along with its causes and effects, is in some extent documented in this book.

In what follows, we do not claim to represent the village in its entirety, or to offer any authoritative claim on its past and its future, nor do we aim to come up with a blueprint for community engagement. What we present instead, is the result of a common effort to address the past, and its manifold importance in the present. Our own vantage point, from archaeology, social anthropology, history, art research and heritage studies certainly puts this concern center stage.

But, equally powerfully, the working-through of the past is the main element of the resilience of this social group, and a lasting source for the creation of personal and group identity and pride of place. We have tried in this book to make our position toward such engagements with the past as visible as possible, to show how our own disciplinary terms shaped the content of research and engagement in the field, in continuous dialogue with the desires, hopes, knowledge and limitations of this rural community and also to point out how our epistemological positions were shaped, and transformed by the community itself.

There are aspects of this work that cannot and will not be made explicit here. Many aspects of ethnographic fieldwork, and, most of all, the affective content of relationships in the field still remain largely invisible to academic publishing norms. Our presence in the field has become over the years a mainstay in the life of locals. A multiplicity of sometimes extremely complex relationships has developed. While we take upon the rather ungraceful task of deconstructing some of these for the sake of understanding, our engagement also has an aspect that maintains an affective load that cannot fit into the demands of academic writing.

To this end, we need as a token of our gratitude, to acknowledge the unseen writers of this book, people who have been as active in its creation as we have been. Kalliopi Markogiannaki, Christos Panteris, Anastos Athanassakis, Eleni Kotsifou, Vassilis Michalakis and Manolis Nathenas have been a constant source of knowledge and guidance. Similarly, Dimitris Panteris, his wife Eva and her mother Eleni have rendered their constant support and inexhaustible trove of histories to the service of the project. Giorgos and Eirini Markogiannaki have been our perennial hosts, to whom our gratitude is immense. The president of the village, Giannis Panteris, and the president of the cultural association, Nikos Markatatos were parts of our project from its inception, without whom this work would not have existed at all. Giannis and Maria Ftenou supported us at the initial stages of the summer school, and Zoi and Manolis Athanasakis honored us with their hospitality during the last few years. We would also like to thank Dimitris Panteris (Petromitsos), Vassilis Nathenas, Giorgos Kotsifos, Dimitris Klinis, for always being there in conversations, activities and celebrations. Our biggest gratitude goes to the community of Gonies in its entirety, and there were so many people we spoke or connected with during all these years, it is difficult to single out the few that can be included in this short text.

Big thanks also to the workers at the day center for elderly people in Gonies, and especially Vaggelio Chnaraki for her collaboration and overall contributions to the project.

This book has profited academically from conversation in and out of the field. We are hugely grateful to Celine Murphy for her contributions to the research and teaching in the field. Vasko Demou was an active participant in the initial stages of the research and has also read and commented on early drafts of this manuscript. Katerina Konstantinou was instrumental in taking this research and engagement a step forward and has contributed to the shaping of this book. We would also like to thank Alexia Karavela for creating a wonderfully rich artistic space in the village, and Vassilis Politakis for honoring us with his craft and knowledge. Participants in the summer school for archaeological ethnography were also a treasure trove of ideas, enthusiasm and quality research, which has shaped the ways we see things in the field. So we are indebted to all of them: Rebecca Ficarro, Carmen Talbot, Nikki Waltrich, Tiffany Campbell, Artemis Anagnostopoulou, Vasilis Balaskas, Alexander Skarlatos-Currie, Alyssa Mendez, Konstantinos Klarnetas, Xanthippi Kontogianni, Ilaria Rosetti, Nevena Markovic, Viktoria Liepkova, Carlos Miguel Silva Canessa, Maria Fouraki, Maria Sarmiento, Marcelo Miranda, Reema Islam and Iraz Alpay.

Parts of this work have been presented in international meetings, discussed in informal group meetings and have been published in different iterations in academic journals. We are grateful to the colleagues who commented on earlier presentations and to the editors and peer reviewers of published articles. They have contributed greatly to the shaping of the ideas and methods described in this book, but of course we claim the sole ownership of all our mistakes.

Introduction

This book is the reflection of a long process of community engagement and collaborative research that began in 2011 as an archaeological project, investigating three Minoan peak sanctuaries in the mountainous area of Malevizi, in central Crete (Kyriakidis 2019). What follows is a record of the transformation of a regional archaeological project into a community-bound, collaborative archaeological ethnography project through constant consultation and engagement with a local society. In this process of transformation, the ethnographic aspect was strongly pronounced, both as an integral part of archaeological research itself, but also as the creation of a social space for the communal creation of knowledge. The initiation of ethnographic research was not solely a decision on behalf of the main researcher, but also the result of pressure from locals themselves, as will be further elaborated in the chapters that follow. Successive seasons of ethnographic fieldwork, beginning in 2011, found Aris Anagnostopoulos staying in the village for several weeks every year, outside the research seasons of the archaeological team. The need to take a step further from the established model of the lone ethnographer who studies a community of people and transform this process into a more collaborative method of knowledge creation that could furthermore train heritage 'experts' in the field, finally led us to set up an international summer school in the village, entitled "Engaging local communities in heritage management through archaeological ethnography." The summer school ran for five consecutive monthly seasons, from 2014 to 2018. The archaeologist and museologist Lena Stefanou, and the archaeologist and visual artist Celine Murphy, a member of the original excavation team, were instrumental in creating open spaces for the creation and dissemination of knowledge in ways that gradually involved an ever expanding group of locals.

DOI: 10.4324/9781003259367-1

The questions that thread through the chapters that follow is how local knowledge, practice, history and memory are turned into heritage, how 'experts' are involved in this process, and how we can help communities acquire greater control of the creation and management of knowledge about their own heritage. Ethnographic research in a self-reflexive mode enables us, we hope, to lay open the theoretical and practical assumptions with which we came to the field, to describe the context within which they functioned, and to discuss the issues, successes and shortcomings of methods we put to work with various communities of interest in situ. At the time of writing these words, we do not have the prerogative of retrospect on a finished project. We are writing instead from the embedded and engaged point of a project that is developing through time. This book aims to document its progress and describe its constant and sometimes tormenting questioning about methods, approaches, goals and ethics.

We set out to record the experience of engaging a local community in creating knowledge about a heritage site, looking toward a form of aephoric development (Kyriakidis 2019, 119) that is inclusive and community-driven. We try to focus more on the issues raised by this sort of endeavor, first of all to lay bare our methods, dilemmas and conundrums in the field. Second, to show that community engagement is not a determined process of implementing a package of "tools," but an interdisciplinary, stochastic process, messy and dynamic, that unwraps through time with unexpected results. As such, it is also a process that questions the very assumptions with which we begin to work, often changing our initial aims and preconceptions.

In earlier publications, we have put the stress in what we call a "pragmatic" approach (Kyriakidis and Anagnostopoulos 2015) – meaning that, besides our best intentions (to decolonize, to enable the voiceless, to engage groups and people into managing their own resources), our position is still the highly negotiable position of a privileged outsider, enabled, but simultaneously restricted from all sides by institutional, financial and social considerations. Instead of arguing that an archaeological project can liberate the people it works with, we are trying to look at the points of convergence and contention of archaeological and heritage 'expertise', local histories (including histories of failed development, political intrigue, traumatic pasts) and imagined futures that our presence brings forward.

One of our major goals in this project is community engagement, a goal that we adopted as an originally stated demand of members of the community itself, even if those members were the most vocal, representative, or influential. However, engaging a community is by no means straightforward or simple. Questions arise at every step of the process and affective states produce a continuous sense of awkwardness, ameliorated only by the hospitality and good grace of our host community. The questions we pose in the field may sound simplistic or straightforward, but they reflect deep epistemic fissures within the discipline: who exactly is the community we are trying to engage? Why should they engage at all and why should they do so at the pace and form we set for them? What is our position vis-à-vis local and supra-local networks of affiliation, community and decision-making, and how we got there in the first place? Can we talk about community engagement if it only takes place periodically, and what happens during our absence from the village? Does our work reach a point when the community emancipates itself from the project and proceeds with its own ways of heritage management? These questions furthermore inform our ethical commitments that are reflected in affective relationships in the field.

Managing research relations in the field is one of the hardest aspects of this process, and it reflects the level of decisions a research team has to make. We could not help but feel that, at the end of the day, and despite the occasional protestations of locals to the contrary, we were good-intentioned intruders who sought to impose their aims and goals onto the community. However, to make the picture more complete, we were also aware of the multiplicity of roles that we hold for the local society, many of which had had to do with our perceived position of power in networks of knowledge production and dissemination. While thinking of locals as people to be taught of their own history may be a symptom of colonial attitude, thinking of them as powerless, unsuspecting "natives" is equally condescending, and plainly inaccurate, as will be clear in the chapters that follow.

Drawing inspiration from collaborative archaeological projects, as they have been so amply presented and analyzed in several publications, we ourselves originally aimed to make our project a participatory one (Kyriakidis 2019, 15–6). On the way, we realized that the limitations of collaboration are much more pronounced in our case, for a number of reasons that have to do with the structural conditions of our project, the institutional limitations imposed by the Greek state and the hierarchy of archaeological values in Greece, as well as the characteristics, desires and needs of the community in question. More to the point, the issue of collaboration, as we understand it, needs to be based on an initiative of the community itself, and carried forward on its own resources, with 'experts' playing a supportive and mediating role, providing resources, social networks and know-how (Colwell-Chanthaphon hand Ferguson 2008, 5–6). In our case, of a rural community that demonstrates exceptional resilience in the face of depopulation and aging, full collaboration in an archaeological project may be too demanding for the local population in terms of commitment, time, capacities and resources. Conversely, engaging locals in heritage management acquires a different hue, as it is transformed from work within the community to community work. As has been pointed out so often by the social workers dealing with the elderly inhabitants of the village, our project has been a source of inspiration, motivation and, why not, entertainment, for a community that is growing older by the day. The relative merits of collaboration and engagement are therefore precisely relative to the specific conditions of communities and groups of stakeholders.

While our project did not become collaborative in the fullest sense, it was heavily influenced by decisions made by locals and was pushed to the direction that interested them most, that is the more recent heritage of the village. We could not help but wonder whether our expectations of collaboration, based on our theoretical genealogies, were in themselves condescending toward stakeholders involved. As will be discussed further on, there are capacities, styles and cultural implications of collaboration that should be taken into consideration when planning and evaluating a community-oriented program. To expect that people will react in the way we expect them to react to our proposals, activities and events, is heavily inflected with a covert form of colonialism, a special sort of blindness to the needs and capacities of communities of people. Categorizations of collaboration (such as the one offered in Colwell-Chanthaphonh and Ferguson 2008) are well-intended efforts at pushing toward more inclusive practices in archaeology. However, they still retain the focus of an archaeological team and do not ask whether and in what way people really want to be involved in the archaeological process, whether they are interested in doing archaeology whatsoever. To expect that people are immensely interested in our work and therefore they should be directly involved overlooks – or rather, undervalues – much more crucial considerations communities of today have to take care of that are usually questions of their survival. The time, effort and dedication that are given by people and groups to our projects, should be seen as gifts from groups who may not have much to give.

Why community engagement?

Community engagement has been the buzzword of choice for socially aware projects and institutions for several decades now. Involving communities and locals in one way or another in the research process and the management of heritage has become something of an imperative for archaeological or heritage projects worldwide, but also for engaged archaeology in academia (e.g. Atalay et al. 2014; Colwell-Chanthaphonhand Ferguson 2008; Smith and Martin Wobst 2005). Despite the bewildering variety and dissimilarities of heritage and archaeological places around the world, the community engagement aspect seems to have become a common tendency to most.

However salutary and well-intended the motives for this turn may be, the practical application of community engagement often creates more issues than it solves. To begin with, this involvement is not what proponents of community archaeology or critics coming from an indigenous archaeology perspective imagined it to be (e.g. Marshall 2002; Martindale and Lyons 2014). On the contrary, it often comes as a vindication of their main criticisms. Institutions and scientific projects are still very reluctant to relinquish control over the production and management of knowledge, or over the material of archaeological and heritage research. Most of them still regard this engagement as public outreach at best, and an effort to patronize the uneducated locals at worst. From the vantage point of funding bodies and assessment committees, it seems that a straightforward application of established good practices or blueprints for community engagement, and the institutionalization of ethics related to community engagement has resulted in mere tokenism. The critical acumen of so many proponents of community engagement seems to be lost as the movement of transformation of archaeology and indigenous studies is gradually becoming institutionalized (Waterton and Smith 2010, 11).

This is reflected in the tone of much of what is written on community archaeology (La Salle and Hutchings 2016, 164). There is an evident, ever-increasing distance between expectations and pronouncements of research and engagement projects, and what results these efforts glean. Most of the finished reports have a top-heavy emphasis on theoretical analyses and ethical imperatives, to the detriment of the practical aspect of community archaeology. Many of our students in public archaeology and heritage management courses come to us looking for much more comprehensive reports and descriptions, not exactly on what people did but how they did it; an account not only of perceived triumphs but also of restrictions, dead-ends, aborted attempts and other issues involved in setting up and running community-based initiatives. This dearth of analytical approaches may spring from the pressure to publish something more esoteric and theoretical in current journals, in order to demonstrate significant contributions – unfortunately, with funding bodies and academic review boards in mind.

The pressure of contemporary academia to "publish or perish" creates a tempo for publication that is inimical to the slow and gradual temporality of community projects. Work with a group of mostly elderly people is a time-consuming effort that far exceeds the budgeting horizon of many funding bodies, as well as the publishing horizon of academic institutions. Moreover, the notion of final "deliverables" of each field season or the project overall, and the implied expectations, are often foreign to processes like the one analyzed here, as the project was ongoing and frequently deviated from our initial aims, being guided by community suggestions and/or demands. Thus, results from a collaborative project may begin to appear several years after the project is initiated; they may be subtle and imperceptible, albeit profound and lasting; they may not be quantifiable enough, or adequately visible in social media or other platforms to satisfy funding bodies and assessment panels.

Additionally, there is the expectation from funding bodies and institutions to get "the good news" on the ethical commitments of the projects they support. This has resulted in an increasingly positive language, that seeks to identify the good aspects of community engagement and downplay points of friction, potential areas of debate, criticism or straightforward disillusionment (La Salle and Hutchings 2016, 165). Simultaneously, managerial culture has introduced an increased need for quick fixes for social issues in the field. This drives many projects to simply include a community aspect in which practitioners go through the moves in the time allocated, without any prospect for truly collaborative work, even on a scale much smaller than the one proposed to funding bodies.

This picture is further complicated when one considers the current climate in academia, where indigenous voices are slowly but surely gaining a foothold to express grievances against a political situation that seems to degrade globally toward regimes of exclusion for minorities, people of color and marginalized groups (Smith and Martin Wobst 2005). Gradually but surely, the established research relationship of subject and object in the social sciences implodes, crushed by its colonial assumptions, its collusion with power networks and its complicity in the oppression of indigenous peoples. Plainly put, the tacit agreement at the core of such research is that indigenous peoples are unable to forge their own future because they are worthless, lazy and dependent (Smith 2012, 4). Conversely, decolonizing projects assume the responsibility to facilitate and advocate for forms of resistance from within the spaces of colonization, to bring stories and communities to the fore in order to achieve social justice. Within archaeology, decolonizing efforts have started to carve their own ground within already existing calls to employ archaeological research as a tool to achieve social justice and equality (for examples, see Atalay 2012, Bruchac et al. 2010, Nicholas 2010, Smith and Martin Wobst 2005).

In this context, the ubiquity of the term community in heritage studies becomes a vexed entity that is not the fast solution to social problems, but an entity that needs to be explained in itself (Alleyne 2002, 608). Fieldwork in this context problematizes reified and non-reflexive notions of communities as homogeneous collectives, marked or defined by common identity traits (Waterton and Smith 2010, 5). It has the capacity to present a fuller picture, where groups of people, networks of power and distribution, national and international institutions and market forces shape an ever-shifting cloud of loyalties, strategies and futures that influence the way the past is understood and managed in the present. In our case, our continued presence and the insistence on collaborative research brought to the fore groups and individuals, as well as discourses and places, that did not feature so prominently, if they did at all, in established narratives of local heritage. As will be discussed in chapters that follow, the creation of co-creative spaces affected something that cannot be done through argumentation and criticism: it enabled those groups to make their versions of heritage heard on an equal par with versions closer to what Laurajane Smith calls Authorized Heritage Discourse (Smith 2006, 300).

...and most importantly, how? Ethnographic considerations

The main difficulty in shaping a coherent vision for community archaeology on a scale that is relevant worldwide is the bewildering variety of its subject, as indeed for all public archaeology (cf. Merriman 2004, 5–8; Okamura and Matsuda 2011, 5–7). While the notion of community is usually taken to be self-explanatory and evident, practitioners in the field address a multiplicity of groups and stakeholders, in a variety of cultural, national and institutional contexts. Additionally, community projects are implemented by teams, institutions or individuals that are wildly divergent in scope, methods, resources and goals. What is self-evident after all is that a university project forging community engagement in Latin America, for example, will face completely different issues and turn out altogether different in scope and function than a museum-implemented program in the Balkans, to take two hypothetical examples.

What is more, examples of good practice in community engagement and participation travel rather badly. What may be valid and ethically motivating in one setting may be unsuccessful in another. To endorse the claims of native Americans to biological continuity and therefore rights over the burial lands of their ancestors may be a salutary move of anti-colonial strategic essentialism. Conversely, to support the claims of Greek locals in the continuity of their stock from ancient Greeks may strengthen ideas and practices that can be exclusionary and essentially racist. Indeed, notions of autochthony, identity related to land, or claims to a shared genetic identity are spelled out very differently and pose profoundly different ethical questions in different contexts around the world (cf. Colwell and Joy 2015, 122). It is evident that community archaeology is situated, context-specific and contingent upon social, historical and cultural factors. While most practitioners may agree on general principles, such as the improvement of the livelihood of communities, the righting of social inequalities, the struggles against colonial domination, there is not, nor can there be, a blueprint for community practices valid worldwide.

Our answer to this conundrum, is to propose a method of research that is at the same time situated in the field and emergent; research that not only documents, but also collectively creates the situations for the evocation of knowledge, empowers locals and situates the research itself in a reflexive manner (Castañeda 2008, 38–9). Instead of presenting heritage work and community engagement as something that is always bound by specific deliverables, we focus more on process itself (Anagnostopoulos and Kyriakidis, forthcoming). It is the process that should interest us more, if we have clear goals about inspiring and enabling local communities to do things for themselves, rather than perpetuating a dependence on our projects, our funds and our initiatives. This approach may create doubts or reactions as to whether our research goals and our topics of negotiation are clear from the start to ourselves and to the communities we are working with. However, as we shift priorities from the expected annual research theme to the process of engagement itself, we thus free ourselves from any academic constraints and expectations and we are able to listen more attentively to what the community wants and why, immersing ourselves into the ethnographic process.

Central to this project is the archaeological ethnography aspect (Hamilakis 2011; Hamilakis and Anagnostopoulos 2009; Kyriakidis and Anagnostopoulos 2015; 2017). Defined by some of its proponents (Hamilakis 2011; Hamilakis and Anagnostopoulos 2009) as a transcultural, multitemporal meeting space for a variety of disciplines and peoples over the chief concerns of materiality and temporality, archaeological ethnography sets up a dialogue between 'experts' and 'non-experts', that is initiated and facilitated by engaged, long-term anthropological research in the field. As a constellation of methods from archaeology and anthropology, archaeological ethnography shifts decisively toward the dictates of anthropological fieldwork, by claiming that the creation of meaning through different emphases on the material and temporal aspects of the past needs to be placed in a broader social context. In plainer words, although we place our emphasis as researchers on the materializations of the past in the present, we need to understand their importance in the context of the livelihoods of the people we study with. Drawing back the focus, we can better conceive of the intimacies of the past not only as phenomena of the local that we come to study, but as constellations of emergent knowledge that become invoked through collaborative research.

This primary concern is materialized in this book in two ways: first, in that this is more an ethnographic account of our presence and activity with a mobile and shifting group of people, rather than a purportedly accurate description of a situated village community. It describes more what we did, how and why we did it in a shifting social context, rather than claim that we, the 'experts', arrived in the field with a defined set of methodologies which we then applied in various degrees of success to hapless villagers that were "there" all along. Second, this account may turn its attention to areas of social and communal living that may initially seem indifferent to a dedicated study of the past in the present: gendered divisions, storytelling and myth, walking and animal husbandry may at first seem irrelevant to an account of how a community of people understand the ancient or more recent past. However, as we hope will become obvious, it is precisely those seemingly unconnected ways of life that become vectors of an indigenous, sensuous and affective understanding of the past with which we engage in the first place. It is this level of connection of everyday livelihood with the conceptualization of the past that escapes the epistemological preconceptions of most heritage 'experts'.

Our approach is inscribed into an ever-strengthening trend toward engaged scholarly practice that aims to make research a public issue (Mullins 2011, 235). Characteristic of such practice evident in what follows is an emphasis on the politics of collaboration within power networks, all the while examining in a reflexive manner the "concrete contours of engagement" (Mullins 2011, 235). What follows is therefore a description in analytical terms of our archaeological project's involvement with a local community and the changes this brought about to both the project and the community. Our choice in doing so was dictated first of all by our need to reflect on our very choices in the field and our need to provide comparative material for similar projects globally. This book, therefore, and its companion volume (Kyriakidis 2019) constitute book-length studies of a community archaeology project that focuses more on the practical side of doing community engagement, rather than theoretical descriptions of what should be done. In striving for these goals, this book delves into some depth in the particularities of the place and its people, as well as those of the project, and the social context in which the production of knowledge about the past is created.

The second aspect of archaeological ethnography that was put in place in this project is the long-term, multimodal and multisited research. We have already pointed out the depth of this particular research project in time. Yet, the need for multimodal and multisited research may seem less intuitive to heritage 'experts'. By multimodal we refer to the developing tendency in ethnographic and social research to delve into a broad variety of creative methods that focus on collaborative and community controlled knowledge creation and circulation (e.g. Chin 2017; Collins, Durington and Gill 2017). As such, multimodal work can employ aesthetics and creativity as a way to trace "ways of knowledge that resist translation" (Grimshaw 2011, 248) in the acceptable ways in which 'expert' knowledge about heritage, for one, is transmitted. The projects described in this book may be considered as examples of what Chin calls "participant making" (2017, 541). Instead of us, as 'expert' researchers, examining, recording, and therefore defining, a community of people, or "discovering" knowledge in the field, there was instead a continuous process of making knowledge into the forms of paths, exhibitions, workshops and open artist studios with the residents of the place we worked in. These processes, described in detail in what follows, were also inventions of how heritage can be communicated to visitors and creatively engage new publics (cf. Powis 2017, 359).

Furthermore, the understanding of a "site" in archaeological ethnographic research and action is greatly transformed by recent developments in communication and the increased mobility of populations and goods on a global scale. The materiality of the past is dispersed nowadays in a multiplicity of sites, institutions, networks and is reproduced, inscribed and reinscribed with meaning, in a variety of media. Therefore, a focus on a specific, delimited space such as a museum or an archaeological site, may not be adequate to comprehend the multifarious manifestations of the past in the present. For even a small place such as Gonies, there is surprisingly ample engagement in national and supranational networks of information and power, that problematize its existence as a "local" place, as a small, out of the way, pastoral village. Additionally, as we point out in the chapters that follow, it is impossible to understand the implication of such places in the political economy of archaeological finds if we do not shift the focus toward more central places where hierarchies of value are created and imposed.

This is another aspect of what archaeological ethnography generates, in that it shifts the emphasis decisively on the politics of the past in the present, that can be a palliative of the simplifying, instrumental approaches that are common in heritage management. The political, with a small p, runs throughout this research and this book, explicitly or not. It stresses the ways in which the material and immaterial aspects of the past play out in struggles over personal and group identity but also shape the ways in which current concerns over the even and equal use and distribution of resources turn into action. Besides the active use of archaeological politics to define community borders or defend communal land, there is another aspect in which the management of the ancient or more recent past constitutes contested spaces for the negotiation of identities.

We have proposed, in this and other works (Hamilakis and Anagnostopoulos 2009; Kyriakidis and Anagnostopoulos 2015; 2017) that ethnography is not simply an add-on to existing archaeological research, but an integral part from its inception. This does not mean that action in the field must wait for ethnographic research to be completed in order to begin. First of all, because this kind of research is never finished in itself, and second, because ethnographic research is not any more a fly-on-the-wall observation of people and places, but instead an engaged social practice in its own right.

Heritagization processes in the Greek context

The paradoxical situations that arise in the field when these considerations are put to practice is a recurrent theme of this book. The vantage point from where it is written is the Greek social reality after the recent economic crisis. It is a social formation where colonialism has been read either as a tacit past with repercussions to the present (cf. Herzfeld 2002) or a visceral anti-imperialist reaction to the current crisis (Kalantzis 2014). In this social formation, and due to a well-established and authorized version of folklore studies that buttressed nation-building (Herzfeld 1986), rural communities are seen as "traditional" spaces, currently enhanced by tourist development that allows urban populations to come "closer to nature," or negatively as the purveyors of an aesthetic of banal nationalism and as pools of a backward conception of traditional values that serve to mask gender oppression, xenophobia and racism. The ambivalence of this reading is further exaggerated when, especially in response to the current crisis, the village life has been resurrected as a handy utopia, as the simpler life many Greeks have shed in their greedy trajectory to an urbane way of life based on luxury and conspicuous consumption. This reading is a culturally intimate (cf. Herzfeld 2004) theory about the internal evils of Greek society that have led to its economic and social downfall.

At the same time, central to the development of the book is a consideration of the impact of tourism as Greece's "heavy industry" (Ikkos 2015, 13) on the self-perception of local communities as well as their expectations for economic sustainability and their relationship with the material remains of the past. Within this process, local places and archaeologically important sites, become inscribed into a total experience of authenticity and are marketed as desirable sites for foreign visitors. The extent to which this process affects these places as well as the livelihoods of locals is not yet sufficiently understood. But we will not be far off the mark to say that it usually goes hand-in-hand with a process of "heritagization" geared toward potential or perceived economic profit from the tourist industry. Walsh defined heritagization as "the reduction of real places to tourist space, constructed by the selective quotation of images of many different pasts which more often than not contribute to the destruction of actual places" (Walsh 1992, 4). We would add to this, following Harrison's later reiteration, that this process of heritagization turns functional things into objects whose sole function is to be admired, displayed or exhibited (Harrison 2013, 69). Hence, the stimulation of nostalgia, the theatricalization of the past, or the ritual character of history are modes of representation that ascribe new meanings to different historical contexts.

This process has two aspects that we would like to highlight at this point: First, it reflects a wider trend of increase in what can be considered heritage worldwide, leading to what has been dubbed a "heritage boom" (Harrison 2013, 166). This boom is received locally through a variety of media, that shape not only the ways that heritage is seen from small places such as the one presented in this book, but it also regulates the sense of the past that local inhabitants may have. In a few words, the past acquires an additional dimension: it is not solely the vector through which an identity is crafted, especially in an increasingly mobile world, but it also acquires a future prospect. The turning of tangible and intangible entities into heritage comes hand-in-hand with a real or imagined potential for local communities: to attract tourists, to create new jobs and make profit, to revive village communities that have been depopulated through precipitous economic out-migration.

The reality of the tourist economy of Crete is slowly perceived by communities and villages that are out of the usual tourist routes: an economy firmly established around mass tourism, especially in the north coast of the island, and a proliferation of haphazardly built, unplanned and quickly executed small shops and rooms to rent that developed along the routes to major attractions, mostly archaeological sites and amusement parks (Briassoulis 2003, 108–9). Besides the impact on the environment and the landscape, the social impact of tourism, now the major, if seasonal, form of employment in the island, has yet to be accurately estimated. Heritage tourism in Crete has developed either as a quick way to manage the spillover from large developments, or as a conscious effort to counteract the proliferation and detrimental effects of mass tourism on the environment, the local communities and the heritage record of the place. In both trajectories, the sense of the past that is inherent in heritage, as well as the affective aspects of heritagization processes, create complex agglomerations of personal and communal identities, pride of place, aesthetic considerations and power networks, only some of which are touched upon in this book.

Second, but not less importantly, heritagization in other contexts is taken to mean the turning of active memory into an uncritically presented "theme" attraction or a dead object in museums, hence a dead-end street for functional objects or discourses, that can be turned into nothing more that museum exhibits. In the case of rapidly urbanized places such as Crete, with an economy dependent on mass tourism, this aspect of heritage-making is particularly strong. In this context, critiques of heritagization that present heritage making as alienation from the sources of history and experience may be turned on their head. Indeed, Crete is one of the places where notions of "traditional" culture are constantly reworked, reconsidered and renegotiated. The development of the tourist industry in Crete in particular, has been a strong push factor that shaped reiterations of the past, from an increased interest in "traditional" music and research on it, to a reconsideration of architecture, a resurrection of Cretan cuisine, to the development of a dynamic small-scale handicrafts industry. The ways in which this process unfolds are certainly disputable, and its aesthetics and politics are frequently objectionable.

However, for a heritage practitioner working in this context, it is a force to be reckoned with as it amounts to a local theory of preservation, memory and historicity.

Community engagement in Greece and its relationship to archaeology

Finally, we need to say a few words on a frequently rehearsed topic in the literature, namely the vicissitudes and restrictions imposed by Greek archaeological law on projects such as ours (Alexopoulos and Fouseki 2013; Damaskos and Plantzos 2008; Hamilakis 2007; Voudouri 2010). The Greek state is the main proponent of research, conservation and archaeological resource management in Greece. Its practices are geared mostly toward conservation and protection, but have often created friction between archaeologists and local communities (see e.g. Caftantzoglou 2010; Stroulia and Sutton 2009, 127; Sutton and Stroulia 2010, 10). The tacit, if clear, admission of the archaeological law is that the state acts as the safeguard against the threats toward the remains of the ancient past from a variety of sources, but mostly from a public that is perceived as uneducated and dangerous to the safekeeping of antiquities. Therefore, while state museums in particular have implemented a series of public programs, sometimes with great success, there is still little consideration, and perhaps outright suspicion, for programs that seek to engage local communities in archaeological research and the management of archaeological sites. At the same time, the focus on protection rather than management or comanagement reaches a stalemate, given the inability of the state archaeological service to cope with the sheer volume of material and sites to be protected. Perennially underfunded, short in personnel and suffering from the usual bureaucratic shortcomings of the Greek civil sector, the state archaeological service workers invest hard work and sometimes their own resources to what seems a diminished returns game of protection and preservation of archaeological sites.

The resulting image, as will be discussed further in the chapters that follow, is one of state abandonment of archaeological sites and the communities that surround them. Archaeological excavations, especially in sites that are considered less important by official institutions, are usually rescue excavations. Meaning that they last for a very short time and aim principally to record and salvage some of the material on the site. There is no plan for further development, signposting, or preservation of the site, and yet the place now remains an area restricted to everyday life. Usually, the mere presence of an archaeological site is enough to characterize entire areas as zones of protection, prohibiting agricultural exploitation and building, but sometimes even stopping the preservation of existing buildings, or prohibiting everyday activities such as watering a garden or rebuilding a fence. Naturally, communities and individuals react with a mixed attitude toward the archaeological service. On the one hand, the expectations of archaeological discovery run high. The presence of an important artefact or site near a community has a series of perceived benefits, that range from pride of place, inscription on the record of national history, and potential increase of income from visitors and tourists. On the other, however, the realities of archaeological preservation and management of sites, or rather its absence, in combination with the heavy hand of the archaeological law, render archaeological sites into puzzling spaces of abandonment and neglect that signal the beginning of trouble for local communities and individuals.

The archaeological service, and the ministry of Culture at large, besides being the state body responsible for this preservation, is also the major employer of archaeologists nowadays in Greece. Archaeological projects that are not state-run function within a context in which all antiquities are a property of the Greek state, most archaeologists are employed directly or indirectly by the Greek state, and all management plans or strategies have to be approved by the Greek state. However large the employee base is for the ministry of culture, the sheer amount of work involved in the local offices (ephorates) and the number of sites investigated or in need of restoration and protection is so large, that these offices remain perennially understaffed and overworked.

Archaeology and tourism in Crete

Crete is one of the most important destinations in the tourist economy of Greece. Most of its tourist visitors come as part of mass tourist packages, stay in large hotels near the northern coast and only venture near the hotel or on specially planned excursions to small islands, beaches, or important heritage sites, like the large archaeological sites of Knossos, Faistos or Malia. While there is an increasing trend toward more benign forms of tourism and the island attracts a large number of visitors for its other charms, like the local cuisine or the idiosyncrasies of its culture and landscape, mass tourism still remains the strong push factor in the island's economy. How exactly this reflects on the politics of archaeology on the island, remains to be studied in some depth, but the sheer number of visitors to Knossos, perhaps the most important Minoan site on the island is indicative (Duke 2007, 23). Knossos receives nearly a million visitors each year. For the first three quarters of 2019, for example, it received nearly 784,000 visitors, making it the second most visited archaeological site in Greece, after the Acropolis in Athens (Hellenic Statistical Authority 2019).

Besides this, the insularity of Crete as well as the genealogies of archaeological research on the island have led to the creation of a detailed, thorough and resilient archaeological tradition. As Yannis Hamilakis points out, Crete hosts perhaps one of the most exhaustively studied Bronze Age cultures in the world (Hamilakis 2002, 4). Starting in the late nineteenth century, the island was carved up into zones of research claimed by foreign archaeological schools (British, French, Italian, American, Irish, Belgian and so on) (see McEnroe 2002, 61).

All the factors mentioned above create what is a tacit, but evident, hierarchy of importance for archaeological sites in practice: while, thus, in theory all archaeological discoveries are equally important to the Greek state, practical, economic and ideological considerations force a hierarchy of values for preservation and protection. This discussion is necessary to explain the full spectrum of reasons why some sites are left to the elements, while others are zealously guarded and protected. All these reasons, coupled with the resistance of state authorities to grant greater control to local communities, result in the abandonment of archaeological sites that are still however under the strict protection of the archaeological law, and therefore constitute no man's lands at the heart of otherwise vibrant villages and towns.

How this book is written: chapter outline

Much of our work in the village is aimed toward recording, collecting, creating and sharing narratives from below. This is not a preservationist reflex, but it is part of a larger epistemological conviction that academia is not the only space for the creation of knowledge and that academic accounts can only be enriched by a sustained conversation with other sites of knowledge production. And a first step to this conversation comes with the recognition that a great part of this knowledge comes in the form of stories, collectively or personally performed. In the contact zones between 'experts' and locals in the field, story-telling becomes an intentional exercise that does not provide ready-made solutions or claims to representational wholeness, but a comment on the limits of this representation (Nagar 2014, 11). In particular, we do not take these stories to be accurate or "direct" representations of a pre-ordered lived experience in the field, but negotiated histories that develop in multiple contexts and acquire different importance and meaning in every retelling. At the same time, we need to locate ourselves as receivers of these stories and make our interest in them as visible as possible. The practices and social aspects of storytelling in the village are further developed and analyzed in a central chapter of this book in the context of the discussion of storytelling as corporate culture and its impact on heritage management initiatives worldwide. Importantly, this emphasis on narrative storytelling as a tool for heritage management is also reflected in the text, which is full of narratives, long or short. We chose to introduce readers to the site by giving a story that reflects events as accurately as possible.

The first chapter of this book, in particular, is written as a long narrative, taking us on a tour of the village and laying out the basic historical facts. It is also a description of the context within which archaeology and heritage are understood locally. It acts both as an introduction to the book, as the personal narrative used in (Kyriakidis 2019), but also functions on a different level as well: it is our offering of a story that is based on true events, but at the same time reordered and valuated through successive and multivocal retellings. It contains the main assumptions and empirical conclusions of ethnographic work as we would choose to tell it to our interlocutors, adapted here for a wider readership. In this respect, it encompasses a process of ethnomimesis, that is further elaborated and laid out in concrete ethnographic examples in later chapters. Storytelling as a performative activity constitutes the connecting principle of heritage-making in Gonies and structures our approach to setting up collaborative knowledge making processes in the field. At the same time this chapter, as well as the third and fifth chapter, show how telling and retelling may bring about significant changes in the way a society considers and evaluates heritage as well as in the practices associated with its preservation.

The second chapter details the sensuous aspects of the presence and absence of archaeological remains, especially artifacts, it the area, and how these mediate the relationships of locals with the ancient past and the politics of archaeological preservation in Greece. Using an object biographical approach, it narratively follows the trajectory of archaeological discoveries in the field to show that the dialectics of absence and presence, distance and closeness, touch and vision play a significant role in the way archaeology is understood both as a process and as an institution locally. Constructing an ethnographically situated critique of the politics of the senses in modernist archaeology and taking into consideration the restrictions that field archaeologists and locals have in handling material from sites, we describe a community project we designed and implemented during our summer school in the village. Based on the experimental archaeological research of Celine Murphy, this project envisioned creative ways to cut through the restrictions in the handling of antiquities to familiarize locals and researchers alike with Minoan clay figurines. Such creative workshops, we propose, communicate knowledge in multiple directions, as they enrich archaeological knowledge, but also mediate the experience of local societies with the ancient remains of the past.

The third chapter describes in some detail the setup of a heritage path in the area. The path was collaboratively designed through the ethnographic process and relied upon the ways in which both historical and heritage knowledge is mediated through landscape. The symbolic significance of roads, paths, routes is tremendous for the local society at large. The "old road" is a composite figure that connects landscape features with narrative lines, bringing in a profusion of stories and discourses about antiquity, modernity, urbanization, social bonds, animal theft and a variety of other social facts. We therefore look at landscape more in detail, looking at the ways in which these composites of embodied dwelling in the field can be transformed into experience-rich methods of conveying place knowledge. The old road, the route that connects Gonies to Heraklio, the island capital and its largest city, follows closely much more antique routes, and is claimed to have covered much of the "Minoan" road to the heights of Idi mountain, where myth has it that king Minos went every nine years to renew his kingly mandate given from his father Zeus. Visible remains of a much older road, possibly Ottoman, but almost certainly laying on the tracks of even older routes, establish the local belief that king Minos went through Gonies on his way up. This belief, as we are going to see, is deeply embedded in political considerations as they are articulated through the politics of development on the island. Nevertheless, it is not a temporally shallow consideration, but also one that is entangled with a complex history of urbanization, the depletion of the population and the resources of the village, and the gradual abandonment of trades such as animal husbandry that were central to the identity and sense of pride of the local population. Our effort to collaboratively set up a heritage path in the area was a slow and difficult task of negotiating these complexities. At times, we found ourselves in the difficult situation to have to argue for the inclusion of more neglected aspects of heritage, related to populations that are less vocal in heritage decision-making in the village. Additionally, we aimed not at presenting a ready-made path for the consumption of visitors, but to find ways to evoke knowledge, highlight aspects of it, discuss it, and provide the resources and methods to turn it into a narrative.

In the fourth chapter, we analyze notions of narrativity central to our project and to every project of heritage renewal and management that wishes to be collaborative and inclusive. Our take on narrative is not only to navigate the profusion of stories, but to also create safe spaces where performative renditions of narratives from marginalized or under-represented groups can be brought to the fore. This chapter is characterized by our take on ethnographic installations (Castañeda 2009) and zones of engagement (Onciul 2015), and how our experiments in the field yielded results. It describes the rationale, preparation and materialization of an artistic weaving workshop that functioned as a space for the coproduction of ethnographic knowledge. This zone of engagement produced unexpected critical stances on what is considered "traditional" weaving practice, its commercialization, and the role of women in it.

The fifth chapter takes a step back to rethink our assumptions and methods of community engagement as academic archaeologists, anthropologists and museologists. It asks once again the fundamental question of why work collaboratively with a community in the first place. Furthermore, it considers whether the initial decision to start a community project influences the course, the control and the ownership of the final product in any significant way. It examines our definitions of engagement and questions their principal assumptions and expectations as instrumental in shaping collaborative projects in the field. Finally, we lay out a tentative examination of decision-making in the field and propose to re-examine the aims of community engagement in heritage and archaeology in particular as tools for building democratic processes.

References

Alexopoulos, Georgios and Kalliopi Fouseki. 2013. "Introduction: Managing Archaeological Sites in Greece." *Conservation and Management of Archaeological Sites* 15: 1–12.

Alleyne, Brian. 2002. "An Idea of Community and Its Discontents: Towards a More Reflexive Sense of Belonging in Multicultural Britain." *Ethnic and Racial Studies* 25 (4): 607–27.

Anagnostopoulos, Aris and Evangelos Kyriakidis. 2022. "From Community Archaeology to Heritage Making: Ethnographic Observations on Building Collaborative Processes through Archaeological Projects." In: Lena Stefanou and Ioanna Antoniadou (eds.), *Journal of Community Archaeology and Heritage*, special issue.

Atalay, Sonia. 2012. *Community-Based Archaeology: Research with, by, and for Indigenous and Local Communities*. Berkeley: University of California Press.

Atalay, Sonya, Lee Rains Clauss, Randall H. McGuire, and John R. Welch. 2014. "Transforming Archaeology." In: S. Atalay, L. R. Clauss, R. H. McGuire, and J. R. Welch (eds.), *Transforming Archaeology: Activist Practices and Prospects*, 7–28. Walnut Creek: Left Coast Press.

Briassoulis, Helen. 2003. "Crete: Endowed by Nature, Privileged by Geography, Threatened by Tourism?" *Journal of Sustainable Tourism* 11 (2-3), 97–115.

Bruchac, Margaret, Siobhan Hart and H. Martin Wobst (eds.). 2010. *Indigenous Archaeologies: A Reader on Decolonization*. Walnut Creek: Left Coast Press.

Caftantzoglou, Roxanne. 2010. *Sti skia tou Ierou Vrachou. Topos ke Mnimi sta Anafiotika*. Athens: Ellinika Grammata.

Castañeda, Quetzil. 2008. "The "Ethnographic Turn" in Archaeology. Research Positioning and Reflexivity in Ethnographic Archaeologies." In: Quetzil Castañeda and Christopher Matthews (eds.), *Ethnographic Archaeologies: Reflections on Stakeholders and Archaeological Practices*, 25–61. Lanham: Alta Mira Press.

Castañeda, Quetzil. 2009. "The 'Past' as Transcultural Space: Using Ethnographic Installation in the Study of Archaeology." *Public Archaeology* 8 (2-3): 262–82.

Chin, Elizabeth. 2017. "On Multimodal Anthropologies from the Space of Design: Toward Participant Making." *American Anthropologist* 119 (3): 541–43.

Colwell, Chip and Charlotte Joy. 2015. "Communities and Ethics in the Heritage Debates." In: Lynn Meskell (ed.), *Global Heritage: A Reader*. Oxford: Wiley.

Collins, Samuel Gerald, Matthew Durington, and Harjant Gill. 2017. "Multimodality: An Invitation." *American Anthropologist* 119 (1): 1–5.

Colwell-Chanthaphonh, Chip, and Thomas Ferguson. 2008. "Introduction: The Collaborative Continuum." In: Chip Colwell-Chanthaphonh and Thomas Ferguson (eds.) *Collaboration in Archaeological Practice: Engaging Descendant Communities*. Lanham, MD: AltaMira Press.

Damaskos, Dimitris, and Dimitris Plantzos (eds). 2008. *Singular Antiquity: Archaeology and Hellenic Identity in Twentieth-Century Greece*. Athens: Benaki Museum

Duke, Phillip. 2007. *The Tourists Gaze, The Cretans Glance: Archaeology and Tourism on a Greek Island*. London: Routledge.

Grimshaw, Anna. 2011. "The Bellwether Ewe: Recent Developments in Ethnographic Filmmaking and the Aesthetics of Anthropological Inquiry." *Cultural Anthropology* 26 (2): 247–62.

Hamilakis, Yannis. 2007. *The Nation and Its Ruins: Antiquity, Archaeology, and National Imagination in Greece*. Oxford: Oxford University Press.

Hamilakis, Yannis. 2011. "Archaeological Ethnography: A Multitemporal Meeting Ground for Archaeology and Anthropology." *Annual Review of Anthropology* 40: 399–414.

Hamilakis, Yannis and Aris Anagnostopoulos. 2009. "What Is Archaeological Ethnography?" *Public Archaeology, Special Volume: 'Archaeological Ethnographies'* 8 (2-3): 65–87.

Hamilakis, Yannis. 2002. "What Future for the 'Minoan' Past? Re-Thinking Minoan Archaeology." In: Yannis Hamilakis (ed.) *Labyrinth Revisited: Rethinking Minoan Archaeology*, Oxbow Books, Oxford.

Harrison, Rodney. 2013. *Heritage: Critical Approaches.* New York, NY: Routledge.

Hellenic Statistical Authority, 2019. Admissions of archeological sites by month (January 1998 - September 2019) https://www.statistics.gr/en/statistics/-/publication/SCI21/- (Last accessed 20 December 2021)

Herzfeld, Michael. 2002. "The Absent Presence: Discourses of Crypto-Colonialism." *South Atlantic Quarterly* 101 (4): 899–926.

Herzfeld, Michael. 2004. *Cultural Intimacy: Social Poetics in the Nation-State.* London: Routledge.

Herzfeld, Michael 1986. *Ours Once More: Folklore, Ideology and the Making of Modern Greece.* New York, NY: Pella Publishing Company.

Ikkos, Aris. 2015. *The Contribution of Tourism to the Greek Economy in 2014 - Summary Presentation of Key Figures.* SETE Intelligence Report, July 2015. Athens: SETE. http://www.insete.gr/portals/_default/Skins/Insete/meletes/Contribution_of_Tourism_to_Greek_Economy_2014_EL.pdf (last accessed 30 January 2020).

Kalantzis, Konstantinos. 2014. "On Ambivalent Nativism: Hegemony, Photography and Recalcitrant Alterity in Sphakia, Crete." *American Ethnologist* 41 (1): 56–75.

Kyriakidis, Evangelos. 2019. *A Community Empowerment Approach to Heritage Management: From Values Assessment to Local Engagement.* London, UK: Routledge.

Kyriakidis, Evangelos and Aris Anagnostopoulos. 2015. "Archaeological Ethnography, Heritage Management, and Community Archaeology: A Pragmatic Approach from Crete." *Public Archaeology* 14 (4): 1–23.

Kyriakidis, Evangelos and Aris Anagnostopoulos. 2017. "Engaging Local Communities in Heritage Decision Making: The Case of Gonies, Crete, Greece." *Journal of Eastern Mediterranean Archaeology and Heritage Studies* 5 (3-4): 334–348.

La Salle, Marina and Rich Hutchings. 2016. "What Makes Us Squirm—A Critical Assessment of Community-Oriented Archaeology." *Canadian Journal of Archaeology* 40: 164–80.

Marshall, Yvonne. 2002. "What Is Community Archaeology?" *World Archaeology* 34 (2): 211–19.

Martindale, Andrew, and Natasha Lyons. 2014. "Introduction: 'Community-Oriented Archaeology'." *Canadian Journal of Archaeology/Journal Canadien D'Archéologie* 38(2): 425–33.

McEnroe, John. 2002. "Cretan Questions: Politics and Archaeology 1898–1913." In: Yannis Hamilakis (ed.) *Labyrinth Revisited: Rethinking 'Minoan' Archaeology.* Oxford: Oxbow Books.

Merriman, Nick. 2004. "Introduction: Diversity and Dissonance in Public Archaeology." In: Merriman, N. (ed.), *Public Archaeology*, 1–17. London: Routledge.

Mullins, Paul. 2011. "Practicing Anthropology and the Politics of Engagement: 2010 Year in Review." *American Anthropologist* 113 (2): 235–45.

Nagar, Richa. 2014. *Muddying the Waters. Coauthoring Feminisms across Scholarship and Activism*. Champaign, IL: University of Illinois Press.

Nicholas, George. 2010. *Being and Becoming Indigenous Archaeologists*. Walnut Creek: Left Coast Press.

Okamura, Katsuyuki and Akira Matsuda. 2011. "Introduction: New Perspectives in Global Public Archaeology." In: Katsuyuki Okamura and Akira Matsuda (eds.), *New Perspectives in Global Public Archaeology*, 1–18. London: Springer.

Onciul, Bryony. 2015. *Museums, Heritage and Indigenous Voice: Decolonizing Engagement*. New York, NY: Routledge.

Powis, Richard. 2017. Heartened by Iconoclasm: A Few Preliminary Thoughts about Multimodality. *American Anthropologist* 119 (2):359–68.

Smith, Claire, and H. Martin Wobst (eds). 2005. *Indigenous Archaeologies: Decolonizing Theory and Practice*. London: Routledge.

Smith, Laurajane. 2006. *Uses of Heritage*. London: Routledge.

Smith, Linda Tuhiwai T. 2012. *Decolonizing Methodologies: Research and Indigenous Peoples*. London: Zed Books.

Stroulia, Anna, and Susan Buck Sutton. 2009. "Archaeological Sites and Local Places: Connecting the Dots." *Public Archaeology* 8 (2-3): 124–40.

Sutton, Susan Buck and Anna Stroulia. 2010. "Archaeological Sites and the Chasm Between Past and Present." In: Stroulia, Anna, and Susan Buck Sutton (eds.), *Archaeology in Situ. Sites, Archaeology and Communities in Greece*, 1–52. Lanham: Lexington Books.

Voudouri, Dafni. 2010. "Law and the Politics of the Past: Legal Protection of Cultural Heritage in Greece." *International Journal of Cultural Property* 17 (3): 547–68.

Walsh, Kevin. 1992. *The Representation of the Past. Museums and Heritage in the Post-modern World*. London: Routledge.

Waterton, Emma and Smith, Laurajane. 2010. "The Recognition and Misrecognition of Community Heritage." *International Journal of Heritage Studies* 16 (1–2): 4–15.

1 From looking from above to working from below[1]

The small party, armed with pickaxes and pulling donkeys loaded with tools, negotiated the last bend of the steep path leading to the top of the hill, and stopped to take in the surroundings. The foot of the hill was covered in vineyards, wheat fields and vegetable gardens. In late October, the entire area around it was turning yellow in patches between the rocks of the surrounding mountains. What little soil existed was cultivated by the people of Gonies, the village that had just woken up at the foot of the hill (Figure 1.1). This hill they stood upon has a very old name, Philioremos, alternatively explained as "friend of the lonely" or "friend of the sheep". The sense of loneliness experienced up here is distinctive: you can take in the surroundings in broad sweeps (Figure 1.2). But there is something else. Standing on top of the hill, you can listen to sounds from the surrounding valley with impressive clarity: sheep bells, people arguing, church bells and pickup trucks struggling uphill. On your feet, low shrubbery and wild herbs fill the air with a brisk smell. Bright yellow flowers indicate the *amabilo*, a herb that is said to cure anthrax in sheep. This place was friendly to goats and sheep and people, for a number of reasons.

The young man leading the party was lean, round-headed, with piercing eyes, a city person. The president of the village, Stefanos, accompanied him, pointing at things, trying to small talk. Most of the climb was spent in silence. Now they reached the top, looking south toward the villages of Anogeia and Axos, and taking in the imposing volume of Psiloritis. The young man ignored the view as he zoned in on the open trenches that were visible on the ground. With a single-minded agility, he knelt in front of them, touching a protruding angular stone that looks like part of the wall. He then turns to the others. "Here!" he commanded. We begin here.

The date was 10 October 1966. The urbane man that led the group was Stylianos Alexiou, an archaeologist and director of the Heraklio

DOI: 10.4324/9781003259367-2

Figure 1.1 Panoramic view of Gonies from the north. The peak of Philioremos is visible to the right and Poupa is on the left. Photo by Aris Anagnostopoulos.

Figure 1.2 Philioremos peak sanctuary with the snowed-peak of Psiloritis mountain in the background. Photo by Aris Anagnostopoulos.

Archaeological Museum. The president was a tall, broad-shouldered man, Stefanos Panteris, from one of the strongest families in the village. Six workers began digging and carting away the soil. Among them, a man from the village and his nine-year old nephew helped the more experienced diggers. They looked concerned at the beginning. They felt they have done something wrong, overstepped some kind of boundary. No more than a couple of months ago they had started to dig the foundations of the community church of Prophet Elias, and immediately they hit upon ancient walls. The church committee had amassed enough funds to build this church, dedicated to the prophet who, according to local lore, went looking for the most desolate place, as far away from the sea as possible. A sailor by profession, he carried an oar on his shoulder and asked everyone he encountered what it is. He finally settled in the place where the answer was: a piece of wood. Up until very recently, there was but a single church in the village, that of virgin Mary. It was very old, some said that it was built by a Byzantine general, Nicephoros II Phokas, when he ousted the Arabs from Crete in the ninth century AD. The church hosted the most significant life events in the community. They were christened there, they married there, they would be carried there for the last rites when their time came.

As of late, the small church yard would fill to the brink with people every time a marriage took place. Others would stand on walls, roads, rooftops, looking at the goings on. The village had grown in the last decades from the small village it once was. Looking at it from the top of the hill, this much was obvious. The houses of the village looked like a painting of the village history, like a collage of different times. To the east, the cramped *Archontika* (Figure 1.3), the oldest core of the village, with houses built literally one on top of the other. A closely knit conglomeration of houses, passages, rooftops and small gardens, very near the most ancient water source of the village. Once upon a time, it is said, at the place where this village stands was a thick forest. A shepherd had observed his billy goat emerging from the forest with its beard wet. He suspected there was a source there. Indeed there was, and he set up his household around it. This story must have happened thousands of years ago, someone said.

The first mention we have of the village in its current name, Gonies, is from a contract dated 7 March 1271, whereby the Venetian lords Pietro Venier and Giovanni Corner sell a field to Alessio Kallerki. The village is mentioned as "casali Gonee [...] in Miloponte" (Lombardo 1942). Miloponte was the Venetian name for the eparchy of Milopotamos, to the west of the village, a place notorious for the

Figure 1.3 Mr. Manolis in front of the ruin of a house in the Venetian neighborhood of "Archontika". Photo by Aris Anagnostopoulos.

abrupt and insubordinate nature of its inhabitants (Herzfeld 1985, 141; 2003, 285). Gonies, and the nearby villages, stands on a notional border between the eparchy of Milopotamos and that of Malevizi. It has changed administrative seats several times in the past, which makes tracing its history in official documents a difficult task. Giovanni Corner is a central person to our story.

By 1966, another church, the imposing Agios Dimitrios had already been built at the entrance of the village. It was a building that corresponded to the post-war boom of the village, which by then had nearly one thousand inhabitants (Office National de Statistique 1964, 293). The church of prophet Elias would crown this trajectory and establish

Goniote pride of place. The discovery of ancient walls in the foundations of the church put the church committee in grave consternation.
The discovery of archaeological finds often spells trouble in Greece,
for private or corporate subjects alike. The best they could look at
was a protracted exchange of letters and a long wait for an archaeologist from the state archaeological service to come and investigate. The
service has usually been, and still is, overworked and can devote little
time at looking at finds like these. This discovery could well put an end
to their plans.

   But this was not the only reason they were apprehensive. This was
the second time the village attempted to lay down the foundations of a
church only to encounter ancient artefacts in the process. The first time
was before the war, in the late 1920s, when another collective effort to
build a church was stopped on its tracks in unclear circumstances.
Mrs. Adamia was about nine years old at the time. She was playing
with other children of her age when a commotion drew her attention,
and she ran toward the noise to see what happened. A small group of
men had begun digging for the foundations of a church dedicated to St
George, funded by a collection made in the community. In one corner
of the foundation, a small statue was discovered. People said it was the
stoicheió of the church, its protector-spirit. Mrs. Adamia remembers
that she heard the commotion and ran up to the group of men carrying the small statue to look at it. As she recalls the day, she crosses
her hands in front of her chest and closes her eyes. For a moment, she
looks stiff and transported. That's how the statue looked, she says.
How big was it? I ask her. About this big, she says, spreading her hands
to shoulder-width. Looking at the length indicated by her hands, the
statue must have been much later than Minoan. Yet, we have to think
back to the shoulder width of a nine-year-old and imagine a much
smaller statue, and therefore a much earlier one. What happened to
the statue? We ask. Nobody knows. It is lost in time, just like the project of building St George's church. At the place where it was supposed
to be built, right above the village, there is an open area, filled with the
red soil characteristic of *Poupa*, the other hill that flanks the village
to the east. This is known as *kokkinochomata*, red soil, without even a
mention of St. George.

   A decade before the Goniotes picked up their axes to start building the church of prophet Elias, in 1955, another archaeologist from
Heraklio had come to the village to investigate a curious find. A local
was digging up the basement of his house to make a cellar and had
discovered a large *pithos* and a stone axe. The bespectacled, lean and
serious ephor of antiquities of Heraklio, Nikolaos Platon, showed up

to look at the finds. Platon did a quick dig and discovered the thick walls of a building which he dated back to Neolithic times, and a copper dagger, which he thought was proto-Minoan. While in the area, Platon looked at several other positions of interest before he returned to the capital never to be seen again in the village. A small paragraph in a scholarly magazine was all that we have from this visit (Platon 1955, 560). The dagger has progressively been turned into a full armor in local lore. This is the *archontika* after all and surely the local lord was a knight of some sort. Looking inside the basement of the modern house, the pithos is still visible, built inside the wall. This particular corner is a convergence of a series of successive walls. It is indeed difficult to decipher where one house ends and another begins. The remains of a very old wall, that locals say is Venetian, are still visible inside a small garden, packed between this house and the neighboring one.

Looking from the top of the hill to the west, the village houses begin to breathe a bit. Larger houses, some with yards, still built next to each other but with a bit more space in between them, some visible inroads and even the odd square. It is the middle part of the village, corresponding to a period of bloom, by the end of the nineteenth century to the middle of the twentieth. The village went up from about three hundred inhabitants to just over a thousand. Space was needed and new neighborhoods were created. The expansion of the village can also be seen in the new village fountain: laying one next to the other, three successive reconstructions catered for increasing demand for water for households. The "new" fountain is further to the west from the first and oldest one. It was once a small tank lined with stone, with a tiny hole for the water to escape from. It is possible that this construction is late Venetian. Next to it, there is a much newer construction, which was possibly rebuilt in 1939, as a caption in a photograph shows, by local stonemasons. A few steps further lay the current fountain, with a much larger tank, modern stone-capping and ornamental leaves made by a local stonemason, now residing in Heraklio. Before modern plumbing brought water inside most houses after the World War II, women would line up with clay pots in a queue for water more than a couple of times during the day. Queuing up for water was a need for households, but also a social occasion for women who were rarely seen outside the house without good reason.

The expansion in space was influenced by other factors as well, such as the changing modes of kinship relations and expectations. Prosperity would materialize the demands that the sons of the family, especially older ones, would build a house of their own, independent from their father's house, even if adjacent to it. This would see an extreme form after the war, when houses became fully detached, with large private yards. At the same time, increased income would lead to the enlargement of already existing family houses, and profound changes in the livelihood of people. The standard family of the early half of the twentieth century would live in a one-story, low-ceilinged house, with one or two rooms. The floor was packed soil, and the roof was made with wooden beams, thatch and clay that was hammered down during the first winter rains with a stick, to prevent leakage. In a typical household, people and animals, young and old, would share the cramped space in ways that remind modern minimalist urban architecture: beds were wooden platforms high above the ground, reached through ladders, under which the family donkey would be parked, or the loom would be worked inside the rabbit coop. The kitchen was also the parents' bedroom, and the working room was also the bedroom for the children. In much smaller households, everybody slept together. As economic conditions bettered, and urbanization changed social expectations, some families began to expand their houses, usually by adding a first floor.

The workmen on the top of the hill would probably have stared in a pensive mood as they realized that the history of their place went much further in the past than they had heard from their parents and grandparents. Most of the histories of origins heard in the village stopped sometime in the early nineteenth century. Many were stories of forced movement for mythical men who fought the Turks during the last century of their long capture of the island (1645–1898) and sought refuge from retaliation in the mountains. The absence of deep historical memory is not surprising for a place like Gonies. While indications of long-term habitation are rife in the surrounding area, preserved in ancient place-names, myths and expressions, the stuff of narrative history is frequently absent. Elderly villagers, faced now with a profusion of histories and their commercialization as saleable heritage in other places in Crete, bemoan the fact that their parents did not "tell them stories" about people in the past. Such stories abound, however, but they are not necessarily stories that can be told in this context. They concern the violent feats of men in pursuit for their livelihood and in constant struggle over territorial control with neighboring communities. They are bloodied stories involving guns, murders and vendettas, or inexplicable deaths and many near misses (see Papadakis 2001). These stories are controlled by a little acknowledged but existing urge to silence. People do not want to get mixed in other people's affairs, perhaps more so in the past, when families were still strong and well-armed, but even today, when such stories become interesting dinner conversation.

It would be inaccurate to describe the village as a typical shepherd village. The high instances of literacy are remarkable for the area and perhaps the whole of mountainous Crete. School dropout was very frequent in the past. Most villagers have only sat the first two or three primary school grades before being pulled out to help in shepherding or household chores. Another obstacle to the completion of primary school was World War II, as during the German Occupation most of the children, who are now the village elders, dropped out at the age of 7 or 8 years old. When the war ended, they were embarrassed to be in the same classroom with younger pupils, and never returned to school. However, reading and writing habits are prevalent. Young shepherds would pick up every scrap of paper available and put it in their sack to decipher letter by letter in the long stints of mountain loneliness. Personal diaries as well as song-books were very common occurrences in the village, as well as personal book collections. The village cultural association, as well as political organizations after the fall of the military dictatorship in 1974, played a crucial part in this. Looking up the ledgers of the small community library, one sees an active reading public during the same decades. Some of what is considered oral folk tradition in the village, is transmitted through writing, in well-thumbed verse-books that pass from generation to generation as family heirlooms.

Still, for those men working on top of Philioremos, Stylianos Alexiou was the urban, educated man, someone to be respected, and perhaps feared, as a representative of central authority. He was different from them, in so many respects. He was speaking in words that were unheard of to them, but he also showed great interest in their own. He asked questions. How do you call this? What would that be called? Alexiou, besides an archaeologist was an accomplished philologist. His edition of *Erotokritos*, the fifteenth century epic poem that is part of the oral tradition of Crete, is monumental in scope and erudition. To establish the provenance of words and expressions used by the writer, a Venetian noble from Sitia, in the east of Crete, he did research with Cretan villagers. The people of Gonies would have been very keen to share their idiosyncratic language with him, and hear the stories he had to say. Yes, the stories he was telling were thrilling. He located early on during the excavation a "votive table" (*thysiastririo*), purportedly used for the sacrifices of small animals. This rang familiar to his listeners. They themselves slaughtered animals every so often, for food or for sale. So, those people, who lived thousands of years ago,

Figure 1.4 The church of Prophet Elias on the saint's name day, taken from the peak sanctuary of Philioremos. Photo by Celine Murphy.

had something in common with them. Every summer, on the name-day of prophet Elias, the village shepherds offer a live lamb to the saint. The lamb is tied to the bell-tower and put on lottery (Figure 1.4).

A tilted wall stone is now in place near the easternmost visible wall as surrogate for what Alexiou thought was a votive table. Locals refer to it as the "altar", another expression that probably was used by Alexiou to describe his finds in plain words. In the autumn of 2014, Celine Murphy walked up to the top of the hill to inspect the condition of the exposed walls. Torrential rains usually bring finds to the surface, such as broken figurines or pieces of pots. The sanctuary walls were left exposed after the 1966 excavation, save for the part that is now covered by the cement floor of the church yard. Rain and occasional thunder may destroy the walls, and a landslide is not impossible in the unsupported sides. Looking at the "altar", she was amazed to discover a dark brown stain covering it. It looked like dried blood. The mystery was solved some days later. Celine was invited to the local distillery, where raki, the high-proof alcohol drink, is made from fermented grapes. In the feast that ensued, Celine casually mentioned the incident. Everybody laughed conspiratorially when a young local showed her a picture on his mobile phone. He was holding a piglet by the legs over the altar. On his other hand was a knife. "We made a sacrifice", he said, "just like in the old times"; to then add "we were bored, what do you expect".

Fascinated as the people of Gonies are with some aspects of the ancient past of the area, they are even more fascinated by the more recent times and the struggle against the Ottoman army and, later, the German occupation forces. Most of their stories have to do with heroic feats and near escapes, during those times. They ponder on mysterious figures of local heroes and their deeds that are lost in time, allegedly connecting them with local landmarks. They draw much of their pride of place from these local heroes, such as Michalis Vlachos, a notorious brigand arrested and executed by the Ottoman authorities in 1856 (Stavrinidis 1980: 40). A statue of Vlachos, unveiled in 2014 with much pomp and circumstance, now adorns the entrance of the village.

The relatively little attention paid to Minoan and ancient past in the area is not only a corollary of the unimpressive finds but also of the stance that the archaeological service has kept throughout the years. Archaeologists have been here only occasionally. Finds from the area are stored in storehouses or displayed indiscriminately among thousands of other artifacts in the Heraklio Archaeological Museum. One cannot help to think that if the attention of locals to the ancient past of the place is minimal, it is because the archaeological service has showed minimal interest in it too.

Alexiou was probably apprehensive as the rain clouds gathered more thickly on the third day of the excavation. His gaze unintentionally shifted toward the east, and the mouth of the Gonies gorge. An intensely cultivated area with vineyards and fields next to the small river that collects water from the valley and pours it into the gorge, it was also one of the busiest places around. The mountain road to the villages of Milopotamos negotiates the gorge slopes and gives to the north of Soros, descending toward Tylissos. Even in between harvests, this was still the busiest passage for people on foot and beasts of burden, despite the car road constructed on the side of the mountain in the mid-1930s. At the peak season for agricultural production, men and women in droves walked, often barefoot, from the mountain villages of the area to work in the much richer valleys of Malevizi down below. But this area is also rich in archaeological evidence. Minoan buildings, evidence of walls and floors, ritual deposits from various ages of history and prehistory.

That same morning, as Alexiou endured the bumpy ride on the car road to the village, he ordered the driver to stop on a very dangerous stretch of the road. They had just passed the slippery and narrow road inside the gorge, the driver's hands ached from holding the steering wheel so tight. Falling rocks still cause accidents on this treacherous road, and the precipitous drop on his left to the bottom of the gorge probably did not help calm his nerves. The driver must have grudgingly abided only to see the wiry man jump from his seat and dart back to where Spyridon Marinatos had excavated what he called a Minoan Villa, in 1935. The road followed the side of the mountain, but on the right-hand side, looking north, he could discern the river Kafatsis running its quiet course through the valley of Sklavokampos, and the old stone-paved road following it under olive trees loaded and waiting for harvest.

Most of the men making up the small excavation team on top of Philioremos in 1966 would have still been children at the time of this major archaeological discovery happened in the area. Some of them would not have even been born. If they were older, they would have been present at the excavation, but not out of archaeological interest. The remains of thick walls at right angles came to the surface as the car road from Heraklio to Gonies was opened sometime after 1930. Able bodied village men from eighteen to sixty years old participated in its construction. The richer ones paid a considerable sum, fifty drachmas, to get exempt. The conscription list compiled by community clerks is two hundred and three names long, and it is nowadays stored in the village archives. Opening up a road in such rocky surface was hard work. The mountain had to be blasted with dynamite and three bridges in total were built. Two of them were stone bridges, built by local stonemasons. They are still there, supporting the road, a monument to the craftsmanship of these earlier generations that present inhabitants of the village are quick to point to. The marks of this ability can be found all over Crete, testifying to the fame of Goniote stonemasons.

The most impressive find in this late-Minoan building was a heap of thirty-nine sealings, probably fallen from an upper story when the walls collapsed. The sealings were used to secure packs of transported goods. They are intricately carved, usually with scenes of bull-leaping. Similar seals have been discovered in remote places of eastern Crete, in Gournia, Aghia Triada and Zakros. Although we do not know what those seals signified, we can be quite certain that there was a connection between these places. This has led archaeologists to propose that it was a trade point on the route from Knossos to the west of the island. In comparison with the Megaron in Tylissos, some kilometers down the road, this is a sturdy and austere building, with few if any decorations and luxuries.

Marinatos obliquely complained in his report of the slowness of the archaeological service in responding to such important finds. The prefecture engineer had reported the discovery for some time before the service was up to speed. And then the service had to put some of the road construction workers to work in order to get everything done on time. By the time the archaeologist reached the Megaron, the road had moved on for quite a while, damaging a small part of the building on its way.

As the excavation proceeded, Marinatos realized that this was an important site, and demanded the road made a detour to avoid damaging it. The ministry offered some money to construct a support for the road. Interestingly, Sir Arthur Evans, the excavator of Knossos, also offered ten thousand drachmas to its construction, believing the building to be of utmost importance (Marinatos 1948, 70–71).

Marinatos stayed there for three seasons, three years in total. In published photos, we can see his diminutive tepee, probably used as a processing lab, set up next to the remains of the Villa. He very much admired the architect of this building, which he dated near to a thousand and five hundred years BC. In his report, he mentioned that this was the work of "an experienced and smart Minoan architect" (Marinatos 1948, 69). Marinatos was then a tall and stocky man in his thirties, with a tiny moustache and curly black hair. When he arrived in Sklavokampos, he was fresh in his position as director of the Heraklio Museum, which he got after a two-year study in Germany (see Mantzourani and Marinatou 2014, 37). He listened to what the workers said, and he even included an inkling of his foreman in the final report of Sklavokampos, an attribution that was not common for archaeologists of his generation (Marinatos 1948, 68). We do not know how the locals felt about this very educated man. Perhaps his appreciation for ancient architects resounds today in their appreciation for the architectural feats of their close ancestors.

Discussion about building and building materials is frequent in the village. Locally, a form of serpentinite, a very hard green stone is common. It is locally known as *philiorimopetra*, Philioremos stone. The hill of Philioremos is a slice of serpentinite, unique for the area (Kyriakidis 2019, 66). This stone is very hard and almost impossible to work with. It is ironic for a village of experienced stonemasons. We can readily imagine most of the Goniotes who walked up the road stopping to examine the construction and discuss the intricacies of the building with the archaeologist or the excavation workers. Small

Figure 1.5 The last standing windmill of Gonies, and the recently built landscape features surrounding it. Photo by Alessandro Skarlatos-Currie.

groups of people gathering around one or two 'expert' builders, who point and tell, judging the choice of materials and the placement of the stone. Such impromptu seminars are opportunities for the communal creation of knowledge. During the recent repairs to the community windmill in 2015, a group of young men gathered around as one of the last active stonemasons in the village inspected the walls of the conical construction (Figure 1.5). He was quiet for a while, looking and touching the walls at points. Beginning the discussion is the hardest part, one needs to know how to lay down the questions, in a way that does not force the technician to impart all his secrets. At that point, the main issue was with the use of weak stones in the construction. For lack of material, the builders of the windmill had also used limestone, which is very sensitive to rainwater. The man inspecting the wall, a study and muscular fifty-year old, with an impressive white moustache, shook his head with apprehension. This is soap-stone (*sapounopetra*), he said, pointing at the limestone and its wide gushes produced by almost a century of wind and rain. The group of men held their breath almost audibly. Sharing knowledge has a performative aspect that is not lost to the Goniotes. Good craftsmen are not only judged by their technical ability but also by their skill in presenting it in public, in convincing the onlookers of their 'expertise'. Moments of grave silence ensued as he continued looking at the walls, touching a stone here and there, huffing and puffing. The president of the cultural association asked the important question: what is to be done? The man replied: that's exactly the question. It was a hint for the onlookers to start proposing solutions to the problem. The performance went on for quite a while, interspersing moments of tense silence with minutes of animated discussion. After a while, the small group dispersed, without reaching a conclusion. These things take time.

We can only wonder how much did Marinatos learn from local craftsmen and their 'expertise' in sourcing and working the stone. Greek archaeologists have always learned very much from local workers. By talking to them and sharing time together at the dig, they discovered new sites or sources of materials. They established routes and possible pathways that connected sites together. They learned about techniques and methods for restoration, building and excavation. Or they picked up interesting facts about agricultural production, pottery work and animal husbandry that later went into their interpretations of ancient times. Yet, the people imparting that knowledge were scarcely mentioned in publications, if at all. Besides taking material from their sites, archaeologists are often seen as taking local knowledge as well and using it for their own purposes, unattributed.

This is probably why locals have sparse memories of the presence of archaeologists in their village. Just like the archaeologists themselves never mentioned local workers by name, so they are remembered as "an archaeologist", even by people who worked with them at the excavation. A man in his sixties once told me how he, as the nine-year-old described above, accompanied his uncle up to Philioremos to assist "the archaeologist" in his excavations. He was an austere, lean man, he said, who did not talk much. He went and afterward they never heard of him again. Similarly, the son of the owner of the house that Nicolaos Platon excavated in 1955, waves bitterly. The archaeologist took the "armor" he found and vanished. We never heard of him again, nor have we seen it displayed in the museum.

The fleeting presence of state archaeologists had, until recently, alarmed the locals. Archaeologists represent a state authority with a great deal of power over the control of communal resources and, most particularly, land. Land is not simply an abstract symbol of property here. It is, or was, a vital resource for the survival of the community. Struggles over such resources were often cause for bloodied feuds in the past. In the late nineteenth century, a family from the village quarreled with a group of shepherds from the village of Korfes, over the spring of Sykia, which is on the boundary of the two villages, right over the plateau of Pentacheris. The use of the water was a highly disputed issue, which had been resolved officially in the religious court of Iraklio sometime in 1865 AD (1282 H). We know this from a note in the archive of the late director of the Turkish Archive in Vikelea Municipal library in Heraklion, Nikos Stavrinidis. Antiquities are never seen as distinctive from the land they are found in as will be obvious in the chapters that follow. So the relationship with archaeology, official or not, is always mediated through strategies of "soft diplomacy" (Papagaroufali 2013). Such strategies aim to control communal resources, but at the same time regulate relationships with the central authorities in a fashion that is profitable for the village itself.

We were implicated in such a communal effort to control land and resources from the very beginning of our research. The first season of study at Philioremos in 2010 was conducted following a brief consultation with the archaeological service and various locals. The archaeological team lived in a nearby hotel complex and scooted through the village every day to reach the hilltop and begin work. It had little understanding of what Philioremos meant to the sleepy community it saw from rented cars as they went by. But they were soon to find out. In a chilly morning in April, work proceeded as normal, the walls were cleaned, and measurements were taken when they heard the aggressive engine sound of a four wheel drive storming up the hill. At the back were standing some village men, who jumped off as the car was brought to a halt and approached them with a menacing look. The questioning began: who are you, what are you doing here. Permits were shown, names were named, embarrassed silences ensued.

When the issue was finally resolved to some satisfaction, the most diplomatic of the group expressed their final grudge: "why don't you stop for a raki and a conversation at the cafeneio? Why do you just shuttle up the hill without acknowledgment?" It is easy to imagine the conversations that ensued in the coffee shops of the village after a stranger car had followed its unexpected route. The two remaining coffee shops of the village form a vantage point from which local men observe the traffic on the national road to Anogeia and the villages of Milopotamos. Heads turn as the engines of approaching cars are heard, and the cars are followed up on the bend of the road and for some time before they vanish in the distance. Controlling passage is and was essential to Goniotes, and it is deeply embedded in memory traces of the past: controlling the passage of strangers from their lands was essential to a community based on animal husbandry and agriculture. The area west of Gonies is renowned for its reliance on animal theft as a custom that maximizes returns from shepherding and also sustains social relationships of a specific kind (Herzfeld 1985, 47). For the community, this vigilance has also been a connecting social bond between individuals and families of the village (Papadakis 2001, 32).

One of the main concerns of the locals is the viability of the church of Prophet Elias, which is built on the top of Philioremos, adjacent to the remains of the peak sanctuary. It is possible that Alexiou did not complete his excavation and there are still parts of the sanctuary under the cement floor that support the church. In fact, the excavation itself happened when the community decided to build the church there, and remains of the sanctuary were unearthed in the process. The church was already underway in the summer of 1967, when a young expatriate from the village, Tasso Christian, appears on the 8-mm film captured by his father, in front of the church being built. At the time, the dirt road leading to the top was not made yet, and village people of all ages would carry building materials on foot or by donkeys. In the memory of today's inhabitants, the church was a communally built monument, that captures the spirit of cooperation and pride of place of the village. The celebration of the saint's name day, on the 20th of July, is an occasion for Goniotes from far and nearby to come together in celebration in front of the church. The religious rites are followed by a lottery in which a lamb offered to the prophet by the village shepherds is given to one of the attendees, and food and wine is distributed to everybody attending the occasion. This is a ritual that has surely developed in the recent past, and quite possibly in response to the dispersion of the village inhabitants during the 1960s and 1970s. At a time when the village was gradually depleted, this annual festival became an occasion for everybody to meet and exchange news and stories.

This new ritual meeting is something that is not far from what some scholars would call an invented tradition (Hobsbawm and Ranger 1983). Few people in the village would claim that this is a habit that goes back in time, while all of them will acknowledge its importance to the coherence of the community and the familial networks of villagers worldwide (cf. Whitehouse and Lanman 2014, 681). This is another way in which a place of deep antiquity is resignified as important in the life of a local community. And this does not happen because of its antiquity or its reference to a nationally endowed sense of the past, but as a place of ritual bonds that secure communal ties (cf. Nelson-Becker and Sangster 2019, 154).

It is these attempts we must look at in order to understand the symbolic import of places like Philioremos to the inhabitants of the village. In 2011, we held a public meeting to establish the way to proceed in our research in consultation with the locals and locate which areas of interest they were mostly concerned with. At some point in the conversation, Vanghelis asked the question, what is Philioremos to you. An elderly shepherd, then in his mid-1990s, was adamant: "Philioremos to us is everything. We hid there from the Germans, we went there when we skipped school, we took our animals there when they were sick." Here is a place with a great significance for archaeologists because of its antiquity and for locals because of its recent history and its use as hideout and protector for both human and non-humans. The same place means different things to different people; different groups also understand and feel the antiquity of the place in different ways.

At the same time, most villagers understand the clash of the old with the new: when we started asking questions about the church, having in mind to compare the temporal scales of historicity, the most usual reactions were defensive: the two members of the church committee were anxious to defend the village authorities that had made this decision by claiming that "people back then, they were illiterate, they did not know that much about antiquity". This line of defense shows the deep distance between our own approach as archaeological 'experts' and the local outlook, and is representative of a hierarchy of power and values that depends exactly on this 'expertise' and the way it has historically been applied. The importance of material remains of the past as vectors for this vexed relationship will be discussed in the next chapter.

While the ancient past as such is less favored than more recent history in local identity-making, initiating a shift in the direction of collaborative research, there are other aspects of archaeology in the area that make it an important presence of consideration to locals. The Cretan countryside has been transformed by European Union-funded programs supporting "sustainable" agro-touristic development (cf Karafolas 2007, 78; Ray 2000). As these programs have materialized in the Cretan countryside, they have greatly shaped ideas about "traditional" architecture and heritage, as well as they have created very specific notions of the preservation and presentation of the ancient past. Archaeological or heritage work is coupled with externally funded landscape construction in view to touristic exploitation and development. In the last decades, EU programs have thus shaped the context in which local archaeological knowledge is locally perceived as part of the creation of material infrastructure in a local area.

They have also shaped the horizon of possibilities and expectations regarding the distribution of funds and resources aimed at heritage preservation. The demand here is to increase access of tourists to remote areas outside usual all-inclusive tourist resorts, and provide different, more sustainable forms of tourism, such as trekking paths, heritage trails and smaller agro-touristic residencies. In this respect, the demand of locals in Gonies and in the greater area to attract more tourists to their lands is colored by a very specific and regimented economic and social situation.

Archaeology is perceived as a very important attraction for international visitors. There is a common adage heard in archaeological excavations in the greater area: "this could be more important than Knossos". The comparison with Knossos, as already mentioned one of the most visited archaeological sites in Greece, rests not so much on the basis of the importance of the site for archaeological knowledge, but on the interest of international visitors.

Such perceptions of archaeological research are inextricably linked to visions of local development. In 2012, the municipality of Malevizi, to which Gonies also belongs, funded the excavation of the *Koupos* site, in nearby Krousonas in collaboration with the 23rd archaeological ephorate in Heraklio. The excavation brought to light a settlement inhabited from at least the end of the late Minoan era up until the Hellenistic years (c. 1200 BC to 100 AD). The increased media attention created a buzz around the place as well as the decision of the mayor to continue the funding of excavations in the area, first initiated by the community of Krousonas in 1980. In a TV interview, the Mayor of the Municipality of Malevizi, Kostas Mamoulakis, said, "until now, Krousonas was isolated" and expressed the opinion that the archaeological excavation would remedy this by increasing tourist interest in the area with "the projection of the finds in international media", and forcing the state to improve the main road to Heraklio.

Almost a decade down the line, it seems that these visions remained on paper, however there is still a strong conceptual link connecting local development, accessibility and necessary infrastructure with archaeological discovery. As we discuss in the following chapter, access is central to local understandings of marginality. Paths and roads, old or new, become hopeful indications of an end to marginalization, but also spaces of struggles over the control of resources. The community of Krousonas, simultaneously with the excavations in Koupos, organized a "revival" of the "Minoan road" to mount Ida, in cooperation with the municipality of Anogeia, to the south-west of Gonies. This path was visualized as a connection between the two major excavations of the area, that of Koupos and the one in Zominthos, by claiming that they were both stops in the trajectory of the mythical king Minos in his equally mythical march to the top of mount Ida every nine years. The inhabitants of Gonies joined in this dispute, by proposing another possible route that passes through their village, and calling on archaeological 'experts' to weigh in on the discussion in their favor. We chose to understand this dispute in an ethnographic manner, as a struggle over the ideological use of the past as resource of material development, and not only as a disputable truth claim. To establish a 'Minoan path' that completely bypasses Gonies may never be resolved in a scientifically satisfactory manner, but it will certainly affect the ability of the village to participate as a potential stakeholder in this heritage space and the possible developments based upon it.

Collective control over land features centrally in these disputes over the past. Consequently, the ancient and more recent past has been used as a lever in the resistance of locals to the intrusion of new forms of exploitation and development. The area of *Sorós*, for example, a pastureland extending to the north and northwest of the Gonies Gorge, has been earmarked as a potential area for the installation of solar panels by private companies. This development is seen locally as a potentially destructive force for small-scale farms and family-based animal husbandry that depend on such lands and annual subsidies from the Greek state. A significant part of resistance against the massive planned expropriation of land by big companies is based on archaeological knowledge and protection policies. A historical narrative of continuous use of this land supports its preservation against the intrusion of large-scale development. Descendants of Goniote families in Heraklio have published in the local press opinion pieces to testify to this continuous use, while locals recruit sympathetic ears in the official archaeological service to turn these areas into officially protected archaeological zones. These local stakeholders have also frequently turned our public presentations of archaeological work in the area into discussions of the latest developments of this struggle.

Territorial claims between villages and the countryside they control also constitute the context in which such developments are understood locally. The inhabitants of Gonies identify such efforts of their southern neighbors of Anogeia as well as their eastern neighbors of Krousonas as attempts to slowly erode the borders between them and Gonies. These borders are crucial not because they determine the extent of current pasturelands in a still largely livestock economy but also because they could have much larger repercussions in plans to install windfarms around the island, including large areas around Gonies. Both our archaeological work, which is partly work on Minoan borders (see Kyriakidis 2012) but also our archival work that discovers references to land use by villagers in the distant past, become relevant in local disputes over intercommunal borders.

In this context, all archaeological presence in the area, and particularly ours, was and is considered an important factor in the very survival of the community as such. In our long-term engagement with the village, we had therefore to negotiate a number of questions that pertain to the ownership, stewardship and management of archaeological remains, and the relative weight these carry in comparison to more recent artifacts, seen as local heritage. In the chapter that follows, we will begin with a discussion of the uses of archaeological objects in a local setting, and the way in which we wanted to approach this as a communal exercise at meaning-making.

Note

1. The narrative in this chapter is reconstructed from Stylianos Alexiou's excavation notebooks, entrusted to Evangelos Kyriakidis, as well as oral narratives collected from the village and archival research.

References

Herzfeld, Michael. 1985. *The Poetics of Manhood. Contest and Identity in a Cretan Mountain Village*. Princeton: Princeton University Press.
Herzfeld, Michael. 2003. "Localism and the Logic of Nationalistic Folklore: Cretan Reflections." *Comparative Studies in Society and History* 45 (2): 281–310.
Hobsbawm, Eric and Terence Ranger. 1983. *The Invention of Tradition*. Cambridge: Cambridge University Press.
Karafolas, Simeon. 2007, "Wine Roads in Greece: a cooperation for the Development of Local tourism in Rural Areas." *Journal of Rural Cooperation* 35 (1): 71–90.
Kyriakidis, Evangelos, 2019. *A Community Empowerment Approach to Heritage Management: From Values Assessment to Local Engagement*. London, UK: Routledge.
Kyriakidis, Evangelos. 2012. "Borders and Territories: The Borders of Classical Tylissos." *Cambridge Classics Journal* 58: 115–44.
Lombardo, Antonino (ed.). 1942. *Imbreviature di Pietro Scardon, 1271. A cura di Antonino Lombardo. Lat (Documenti e studi per la storia del commercio e del diritto commerciale italiano. no. 21.)*. Turin: Libraria Italiana.
Mantzourani, Eleni and Nano Marinatou (eds). 2014. *Spyridon Marinatos 1901-1974: I Zoi kai i Epoxi tou*. Athens: Kardamitsas.

Marinatos, Spyridon. 1948. "To Minoikon Megaron tou Sklavokampou". *Archeologiki Efimeris* 1939–41: 69–96.

Nelson-Becker, Holy and Kimberly Sangster. 2019. "Recapturing the Power of Ritual to Enhance Community in Aging." *Journal of Religion, Spirituality & Aging* 31 (2): 153–67.

Office National de Statistique. 1964. *Résultats du Recensement de la Population et des Habitations, Effectuée le 19 Mars 1961.* Athens: Royaume de Grèce, Office National de Statistique.

Papadakis, Manolis. 2001. *Gonies. Ena taksidi sto chrono kai sto choro.* Thessaloniki: Ekdoseis Aplatanos.

Papagaroufali, Eleni. 2013. *Soft Diplomacy. Transnational Twinings and Pacifist Practices in Contemporary Greece.* Athens: Alexandria.

Platon, Nicolaos. 1955. "Chronika." *Kritika Chronika* 9 (3): 517–69.

Stavrinidis, Nikolaos. 1980. *Michalis Vlachos. O Teleftaios Chainis kai to Tragiko Telos tou.* Iraklio : n.p.

Whitehouse, Harvey and Jonathan A. Lanman. 2014. "The Ties that Bind Us: Ritual, Fusion, and Identification." *Current Anthropology* 55 (6), 674–95.

2   Objects and object biographies in archaeology and heritage

We descend the platform to the disused underground parking lot. The midday heat gradually turns into a dry coolness and our eyes grow accustomed to the thickening darkness as we come in front of white shutters blocking our way. On the one side, they are cut in the shape of a door. We knock, and someone from inside asks to see our credentials. Soon, the door opens a notch and the moustached man of an eforeia guard looks at us. He recognizes Vanghelis and immediately pulls the door back with relief. We walk in. The place is huge; there are thousands of plastic crates, the ones used to carry grapes to large wine-presses, in stacks that reach to the ceiling, forming narrow passages between them. This must be the labyrinth of ancient legend. One can easily get lost in here, and would be surprised if no one did in the past. Those crates are full with the findings of so many years of excavations on the prefecture of Heraklion. We are inside the apothiki, the storage room of the Heraklio eforeia. A future archaeologist might be hard pressed to understand how all these artifacts came together in this underground storage room; she may speculate some sort of cultic activity, if it is *a la mode* when she works in the future to imagine past society based on religious practice. In front of the chaos of crates and material, an anti-quated metallic desk hosts the two guards. We sign the visitor ledger and proceed to the depths of the storehouse, to a platform enclosed with paneled walls and glass windows, where the situation is different.

From the relative darkness of the storeroom, lighted by neon lamps hanging from the ceiling, to the piercing white light of the laboratory, where the archaeologists of the project are poring over clay finds, cleaning and measuring them, photographing them, recording every aspect of their material existence that is considered important. This is where archaeology happens, besides the excavation site, the library or the public domain. Here, the tiny figurines assume their existence as "objects," separated from the environment in which they were

DOI: 10.4324/9781003259367-3

discovered. They are on their way to becoming artifacts of a culture, signifying objects of the Minoan world. They look so much different here, the context is alien to them. Merged with the clay and stone of Philioremos, they mixed with their surroundings to the degree that they were invisible to the untrained eye. Here, juxtaposed with photographic cameras, measuring instruments, laptops and electric light, they look as alien and intriguing as they could get. This is their entry to a new life, that of the archaeological object (see Holtorf 2002, 50; Trigger 1989, 99; Witmore 2015, 206), and the security measures taken at the door indicate how little 'non-expert' populations can now control or even follow their trajectory.

Before entering this enclosure, the clay items and figurines of Philioremos were available, in a sense, to the people inhabiting the area. They were, and some still are, there in the open, exposed to the elements but also to human intervention. It is not rare to pick up an object that is visibly worked by human hands after a spring shower. They appear like snails after the rain. People do not pay much attention to these seemingly clumsy clay pieces. Besides, it may take keen observation skills to pick out parts of a figurine among the profusion of stone, clay, shrubbery and sheep droppings in the area. In nearby peak sanctuaries, however, the profusion of clay remains is impressive, and the small items, exposed to the elements, humans and animals are protected from souvenir seekers only by the distance and difficulty of reaching the sanctuary.

The nature of archaeological engagement in the area makes these objects a strange affair. Most excavations or surface surveys in the area are "rescue" excavations. The state archaeological authorities have scarce resources and scant personnel. So, even important sites are usually quickly explored, recorded and then left to the forces of nature. Some material is carried away to storage and museums, as already described above, but a great deal may be left in situ, especially on sites such as peak sanctuaries. Peak sanctuaries have been relatively marginal in the development of Minoan archaeology up to quite recently, and therefore the emphasis on their preservation and exploration has been minimal (Peatfield 1990, 117; 2009, 252–3). Simultaneously, the nature of these places, usually lacking in infrastructures and exposed to the elements, makes it even more difficult to collect and record all material in a systematic manner. These factors combined have created an archaeological presence in the area that has been sporadic and eventual. But no real effort at the engagement of locals with archaeological artefacts was made in the past, and certainly there was no effort to inform locals of the future of objects collected from their area.

To understand the lengths to which a local from Gonies must go to in order to locate one such artefact, one has to consider the profusion of material and the curating style of the Heraklion archaeological museum. This is one of the largest museums in Greece, with exhibits spanning many millenia, from the neolithic period up to the Roman era of the island. The recently renovated (2013) museum has twenty-seven large halls, in which a wealth of material is presented in glass displays, placed in chronological order. A mere walk through the museum and a look at the brief explanations offered in each and every display will take up a whole morning. It is very difficult, if not impossible, for the lay person to locate an artefact from a particular place, unless she is taken there by an 'expert'. The Philioremos figurines are presented amongst other similar ones from other parts of Crete in a display several halls down inside the museum. Buried amidst several other similar figurines, it takes a keen eye and prior knowledge to understand where this is coming from – and vivid imagination to place it back in its surroundings or to trace the trajectory it has followed to this place.

While it is difficult to follow an object in its trajectory through the cogs of official archaeology, there are other factors that may kindle archaeological interest in 'non-experts'. The presence of archaeologists like us in the area alters the relationship of locals to ancient artefacts, and highlights objects as anchors of meaning (Scarpaci 2016, 5). This is reflected in the reactions of locals to the profusion of fragmented ancient remains that can be found on the surface of Philiorimos and other sites. A worked tile, a piece of a figurine, a stone tool, are now transformed from mere things into artefacts, that is things tangled in social interactions. They are objects that can initiate dialogue, can enforce or break relationships between people, or people and institutions, they are objects that somehow relate everyday livelihoods to the services of the state and transform living landscapes into places of archaeological interest.

Arjun Appadurai shows how people and things are inextricably tied together in creating the social and the everyday (Appadurai 1986). Objects, he claimed, based on Igor Kopytoff's approach, can have life cycles and biographies (see also Gosden and Marshall 1999). Appadurai further distinguished between object biographies and the social histories of things. One can follow the trajectory of an object in its entry and exit from the commodity cycle, but one can also look at what happens at "classes of things" in longer time spans (Appadurai 1986, 34). Within archaeology, the material culture approach has developed into deeply ethnographic and richly contextual accounts of the role of material things in shaping human worlds (Hodder 1982, 9;

see also Holtorf 2002; Joy 2009). Biographical accounts of things, in particular, have been employed as a rich metaphor to examine the transformation of people and things as conjoined entities through time (Gosden and Marshall 1999). This approach has been expanded by anthropological perspectives to include archaeological sites themselves (Deltsou 2009). In this respect, we may look at what happens at a figurine discovered on the hilltop of Philioremos as it travels to exhibition, publication or storage, and consider this itinerary in view of the category of things called Minoan archaeological artifacts.

The experience of following the archaeological artifact in its trajectory from site to storage or exhibition, highlights the vicissitudes of archaeological politics in the Greek state. Before they become artifacts representative of the Minoan civilization, there objects lead lives in close proximity with human actors, have histories and biographies inextricably linked with those of humans in the area, and acquire their value in a world of their own. In fact, the very transformation of these objects to Minoan artifacts presupposes that they are completely cutoff from this milieu and transported to a completely different space, away from the sight and touch of 'non-experts'. As we have indicated above, such objects may acquire importance as they travel through the stages of archaeological collection and study, but they may also be lost forever in bureaucratic oblivion. Both cases apply to artefacts discovered in the vicinity of Gonies. Figurines from Philioremos are displayed in the Heraklio archaeological museum; and conversely, discoveries collected in the mid-1950s from houses inside the village cannot be located anywhere in the storerooms or the ledgers of the museum.

As Yannis Hamilakis has so cogently argued, the haptic qualities of archaeological material in Greece are very much underplayed (Hamilakis 2013, 45). In fact, it is very rare for state archaeology to allow ordinary people to touch archaeological artefacts. Some would say for good reason, since the hands of 'non-experts' may be destructive to the artefacts themselves, and detrimental to archaeological investigations. On the other hand, however, the primacy of vision as a sense in approaching antiquity constitutes a bodily regime that comes in stark contrast with the way most locals approach ancient artefacts in general. Our way out of this apparent impasse is to devise ways to bring the materiality of antiquity back into the equation, but without jeopardizing materials or the scientific significance of archaeological discoveries.

An artefact is not archaeological as a matter of fact. Its temporality, as duration in time, is, as with every other object in the world, a neutral temporality. To become archaeologically significant, this artefact will have to enter a network of signification. It has to be recognized, located chronologically and attributed a meaning. It has to be recorded, catalogued and named. It then has to be stored, protected with other artifacts of similar provenance. It finally has to be studied, photographed, sketched and published, or exhibited for posterity. All these human actions are what turns a neutral duration of an object into a significant temporality, a representative of an era. Archaeological activity, like all meaning-making activity, entails the transformation of things – in this case, from objects to artefacts. In the example of the Greek archaeological process, this also entails the complete separation of any such objects from their initial surroundings and their detachment from the community of lay people that may have been involved in successive parts of its discovery, study and explanation.

But this also points to another thing: the difficulty of introducing methods and techniques to establish a sensory proximity to the archaeological record. Objects are active agents in human life, shaping spaces, behaviors, aesthetics and sensibilities through direct proximity that engages all senses. However, most archaeological objects in the Greek state's object-scape are things that are removed from everyday life and are solely directed toward the visitor's gaze. This visual construction of the archaeological, both elsewhere but also in Crete in particular, is intensified in the context of an increasingly commercialized tourist industry (Duke 2007, 120; Solomon 2006; Yalouri 2001). Any community engagement project that seeks to introduce more tactile approaches to archaeological artifacts will collide head-on with the legal framework of the Greek antiquities law that prohibits any handling of antiquities by 'non-experts', except on rare occasions.

But why would this sensuous contact with the remains of the ancient past acquire such importance for a project like ours? We believe that a visual mode of presenting object biographies and following object trajectories is only one way of experiencing the past; and, while it may be the dominant one nowadays, it is not the strongest one as far as our interlocutors are concerned. To develop notions of stewardship of heritage, we need to devise ways to promote the sensuous aspects of indigenous archaeologies, while at the same time informing them with the concerns of object preservation, recording and archiving.

Yet, there are other ways of engaging the past with multiple senses, ways that we may devise to be profitable and fulfilling for both 'experts' and 'non-experts'. In what follows here, we are going to present first the sensory aspects of dealing with the ancient past, as we have experienced them in Gonies, and we are going to discuss how an art and experimental archaeology project opened a window to the past.

Living within a Minoan landscape

The elements that constitute Minoan archaeology, an agglomeration of people, things, institutions and perceptions about the past, frame the existing landscape and transform material stuff into significant items. While the area of Philioremos, for example, is important to locals as a communal space, its material culture is mostly undifferentiated to 'non-experts', and part of the landscape to inhabitants of the area, and therefore open to actions that may seem destructive, or even sacrilegious to archaeologists. Many of our interlocutors remember themselves trying to push downhill one or more of the squared stones of the sanctuary in their teens. A game dangerous to potential passersby or flocks, but at the same time a highlight of the long and uneventful afternoons of childhood. Some villagers remember picking up a figurine body, which they transformed into a doll to play with, or finding a complete cup that they saved somewhere among other interesting finds – an eagle skull, an empty bomb shell, a medicine box from the World War II – in storage rooms of their own, compared to the official ones only in their chaotic jumble of different material.

At the same time, however, we must not think that the indifference of locals to such material evidence means that they were not in any way alert to its significance, or that some of these artifacts did not make a lasting impression upon them. One local for example gave us a long description of the clay figurines they discovered while tilling a field in the plains of Malevizi. While describing the figurines, he stood up and imitated their stance with his body, squinting his face to reproduce their facial expression. His shoulders came together in an affecting manner to describe the miniscule size of their body parts, and, when he described their most remarkable feature, their pyramidal clay hats, his face beamed with a broad smile. The same local claimed the figurine he made with us in the experimental workshop we are going to describe below, and promptly exhibited it in a shelf, over photographs and other keepsakes. Activity such as that described by our interlocutor is usually seen by authorities as vandalism and looting. We could however shift slightly our view and see from the perspective of people who develop tactile engagements with ancient artifacts alongside local cultures of collection, to discover that these approaches do not always signify a quest for profit or personal advancement; at other times they represent a rich, if uninformed, quest for fuller engagement with the past, one that deploys more senses that that of vision (cf. Antoniadou 2009; 2014).

Sensuous engagements with the remains of the ancient past are not only part of a public archaeology that seeks to inform the 'non-expert' of any archaeological discoveries more fully. It is also a part of an archaeology that is richer in context and considers a multiplicity of temporal scales. Sometimes, for example, the bodily memory of locals may be the only window archaeologists have to lost evidence of the ancient past. As already mentioned, in another occasion we were discussing with a 94-year-old lady her memories of the aborted effort to construct a church of St. George right above the village. The church was funded by a community collection in the early 1930s, and was to be built in an area that is marked by soft red soil, immediately above the middle of the village. What happened to this project is a mystery, and few people in the village remember anything about it. Our interlocutor, however, remembered being a young girl of almost nine years old, when news of a strange discovery reached the village. She recalled grownups coming down the hill in a hurry, carrying a statuette in their hands. The spirit of the place, she said, there was expected to be one in each corner. In her reminiscence, she remembers approaching the team and taking a look at the statuette. How was it? We asked. Instead of a response, she crossed her hands on her lap, and closes her eyes. For a moment she was transformed to a Minoan statue, the one in her mind's eye. The obligatory archaeological question came next: how tall was it? An answer to this question may have had given us evidence of a very rare discovery, or a peak sanctuary very close to that of Philioremos. She indicated with her hands parallel to her sides. The distance between her palms, those of a grown up, must have been about thirty centimeters. If this was so, the discovery would have been a very rare figurine. But bodily memory can be misleading. The breadth of hands was that of a nine-year-old, which made the artefact much shorter, about the usual heights of votive offerings to peak sanctuaries.

The bodily performance of the memory of material things is one of the avenues through which we can understand better the relationship of locals to the remains of the ancient past. Bodily interactions with the ancient past have been considered a potentially dangerous practice for the preservation of antiquities, especially in the Greek context. Seen from a different perspective, however, the affective load that these materials carry and the wonder of their encounter are strong vectors of any effort to develop good practices of stewardship and protection. The Greek antiquities law ultimately relies on a sense of state ownership and a duty of patriotism to enforce, rather than inspire, good practices of preservation of ancient material heritage.

The reasoning of the law is that, since the remains of the ancient past are proofs of the continuity of the Greek nation from ancient to modern times, contemporary Greeks should preserve these remains as sacred relics at the core of their nationhood. This approach has repeatedly been deconstructed in a rich literature on the subject, so we need not rehearse these arguments further (see, e.g. Damaskos and Plantzos 2008; Hamilakis 2007). The idea that current Greeks are descendants of ancient Greeks may be pervasive in Greek society, but we have already hinted that locals in Gonies do not conceptualize the ancient past in such clear terms of biological ancestry. They do not feel that the people once living where they now live were their ancestors. Although they may feel, in the general framework of Greek national education, that they form part of the continuum of Greek civilization that has been in place since antiquity, they do not feel that the actual remains of the Minoan past in their area are proof of the village lineage extends so far into the past. In fact, the abstract ideal of Greek or Minoan civilization may come in contrast with the feeble material traces that represent it. Their lack of identification brings to the fore an understanding of belonging that may be original in the annals of Greek archaeology. Goniotes feel that they are responsible for the safekeeping of this place, its ancient heritage included. In other words, they have a developed sense of stewardship, which comes had in hand with notions of ownership of this place, as well as a proximity to the land and its resources.

Surprisingly, while this is mostly true of older generations, it is starting to change for younger ones. As the bonds with the landscape begin to weaken for generations raised away from the village and the land itself, the relative weight of ideological constructions of Greek ancestry begins to replace the realities of lived material remains of the ancient past. For younger Goniotes, archaeological heritage is a disembodied characteristic of their village, one that may act as proof of the importance of their ancestral place in the timeline of the Greek nation. Again, as indicated in earlier chapters, heritage becomes dematerialized, exits everyday use values and enters the realm of ideology. We must understand this again as an effort at meaning-making for a place, in the absence of tangible links to the landscape.

This developed sense of pride of place, linked with a bodily engagement with archaeological sites and artifacts and a sense of stewardship could lead to an alternative model of sustainable practices for archaeological preservation. However, we could not help but wonder why several finds such as the ones described above were not handed in to the museum in Heraklio. To interpret this lack of good practices, we have to look at the coexistence of many different factors: first of all, the indifference of locals to these artefacts as archaeological evidence; besides their tactile and sensuous qualities, they remain for the most part unframed, incomprehensible and void of meaning. Second, the difficulty that is associated with dealing with state bureaucracy, and the insignificant returns that any action of stewardship as understood by the Greek state has for the local population. Third, the examples of material that has already been handed in to the Heraklio museum or discovered in excavations in or around the village do not set an inviting course for locals that may discover an archaeological artifact of importance.

Beginning with the latter, it is interesting to examine briefly the best-known case of extensive dealings with the archaeological service. The owner of one of the oldest houses in the village decided to build a cellar in the early 1950s and began digging. Soon, he hit upon what were the remains of a much older settlement. The son of this owner told us that his father called the archaeological service, which is corroborated by the service archive. Nikolaos Platon, then ephor of the Heraklio museum, performed a quick rescue excavation. The son of the owner related it as follows: "they dug the floor and discovered walls, pots, a sword and a whole armor. They took them away and we have not heard of them since. We do not know where they took them." A suspicious tone underlined his musings. Indeed, the meagre artifacts that were discovered in reality and included in Platon's report the following year (Platon 1955), were transformed by their absence into much more glorious discoveries; discoveries, it seems that were worthy of being hidden somewhere and not mentioned of again. It seems to us that it may be pointless to try to convince anyone with this experience of handling antiquities to keep up any sort of good practice regarding any remains of the ancient past. There seems to have been no effort of communicating the discovery back to the locals, and none would have been expected of Greek archaeologists in the 1950s. Platon's excavation was briefly mentioned in a report published in a locally published scholarly journal, Kritika Chronika, and did not make its way back to the village as far as we know. Even so, it may have been incomprehensible to the locals with all its technical language and contrived syntax.

In an effort to rectify this lack of communication, we included a reproduction of the paragraph where Gonies are mentioned in Platon's article in the public art installation we made in the village in 2014. We framed the reproduction in a conspicuous orange frame and placed it on a prominent wall in the small square, very near where the actual discovery happened. We intended this as a trigger for further discussion and exchange of information, as well as a way of giving back to the people concerned what should have been given some decades ago. The installation prompted discussions of the material concerned, which gave us the opportunity to clarify what exactly has been discovered and handed in – at least according to Platon's report, because the actual finds are, to all terms and purposes, lost in the meandering halls of the museum storage rooms. It also enabled us to begin a discussion on good practices regarding the handing in of archaeological evidence.

Our presence and continuing discussions in the village has changed the attitudes of locals toward archaeological discoveries. Through our activities, workshops, discussions and mere presence, the value of archaeological artefacts has been transformed, while incorporating the sensuous qualities that locals engage with. More importantly, however, through workshops we devised and put into practice, we managed to make spaces where locals and 'experts' would meet and exchange information and knowledge, while engaging with the materiality of ancient artifacts on a very different register.

Making spaces for collaborative creation

In the summer of 2015, we setup in the field a month-long public archaeology project with our collaborator Celine Murphy. Celine's work on Minoan figurines has developed an experimental archaeology aspect, in which she has tried to recreate the techniques used in figurine making in Minoan times (for results from this approach, see Murphy 2020). Part of her work is to ask different audiences to reconstruct a figurine based on observations on the method of construction on remaining figurines. In collaboration with Vasilis Politakis, an 'expert' potter from Heraklio, we issued a public call for participants in this workshop. Spanning four weeks, the participants would first be instructed on how clay deposits are located by archaeologists, and how to differentiate clay deposits from the soil surrounding them. Participants in the workshop, both from the village but also from Heraklio, collected clay from known sources in the area, and then brought it back to the community building to clean, grind and store for later use. In the second meeting of this workshop, the cleaned and sieved gray dust was turned into workable clay.

After consultation with local participants (Figure 2.1), two groups were formed: one group joined Celine in making Minoan-like figurines, and another group made things out of clay that were significant to them. The figurines group issued results that were very useful for the

Figure 2.1 Planning the clay workshop in one of the coffee shops of the village. Photo by Aris Anagnostopoulos.

archaeological team: it rendered further support to the hypothesis that figurines were not easy to make, but required some sort of specialized knowledge. In the past, based on the primitive characteristics of figurines, and their crude form, archaeologists proposed theories that these were constructed by everyday people, with little or no knowledge of how they were made, possibly imitating already existing ones. The experimental aspect of this project has offered indications that this picture is not entirely accurate. In fact, figurines must be constructed in a very specific way, one part after the other, before they are joined together and baked in a kiln. Legs, for example, must be constructed first and left to dry for a while, so that they can support the upper body, added later. All this was explained as locals set about to create their own figurines.

Transforming clay in a way that someone may have done more than three thousand years before our day was a fetching experience for those participating (Figure 2.2). It made them aware of the complexities of constructing figurines, and opened a different perspective to the figurines as objects. Touching and forming a figurine from unformed clay has bequeathed to participants a bodily memory of touching the wet clay, shaping the body and head, adding the eyes. When participating

Figure 2.2 Participants gather around the tables at the clay workshop. Photo by Aris Anagnostopoulos.

locals now look at an original Minoan figurine, they think of it as an object of tangible material memory, as something they themselves are able to construct and have done so. It thus adds a level of proximity to this object, enhances its value in experiential, and not economic terms, and strengthens the sense of stewardship that the local community feels toward the archaeological remains of the past.

During the construction of figurines, a local coffee-shop owner decided to make a statuette of his own. He has followed many professions in the past, including that of stonemason, and he owned a workshop constructing alabaster objects for some time in the 1980s, catering to the booming tourist trade of the era. Drawing on his skills as an experienced stonemason, he created a female form that incorporated many elements that could be said to harken back to an ancient motif (Figure 2.3.). Minimal characteristics, hair drawn back, armless torso, all were expressive features of an artist's aesthetic approach to the past, as well as a reflexive commentary on the workshop we were running. After the figurine was fired, Dimitris claimed it and it now adorns his coffee shop. We could approach this unexpected creation in our workshop as an unwitting commission of a local artist that we were not aware of before. The workshop itself opened an avenue for expression of this artist, who offered a commentary on popular perceptions of the ancient past, pottery and clay-working, and modern renditions of ancient vestiges.

Figure 2.3 A female form created by a local participant in the workshop. Photo by Aris Anagnostopoulos.

Ethnographic research is mostly based on words exchanged either in written or oral form. Comments such as this are difficult to convey in a way different than what we are now doing, nothing short of explaining away the totality of this artwork. The workshop alerted us to alternative, multimodal ways of framing archaeological experience. The local cultural association was also alerted to the possibilities of such an endeavor, opting to keep the figurines created during our workshop to make them a permanent exhibition in the community school at some future date. Furthermore, this practice alerted us to the value of offering avenues for the expressivity of locals in different things and material objects.

Two ladies participating in this workshop decided to show us how they made clay objects to play with when they were children (Figure 2.4). Proceeding carefully and methodically, as embodied memories slowly came back to them, they produced a series of small pots, trays and bread loafs that they made in the past to recreate household visits, lacking any toys to play with. They did this despite the persistent nagging and freely offered comments by male observers, who commented on the crudeness of their pots. The fact that women of their age were participating in such an event was considered somewhat problematic, that they should have been in the kitchen cooking lunch at this time of the day, etc. They responded kindly, establishing their position there and claiming their right to produce the artifacts they made.

The baking of these clay artifacts was then made out in the open, in a specially constructed open kiln, made by Vassilis. The construction and firing of the pot turned into a communal process, in which many persons offered their opinions, ideas or contributed manual work. Local stonemasons helped in constructing the sides of the kiln, a bulldozer operator from a neighboring village was called to dig the shaft, the municipal fire extinguishing vehicle was manned by us and the village authorities, and many villagers were either looking on the process or guarding the surrounding area for stray sparks. The firing of the kiln was turned into a village celebration, with the obligatory lamb sides cooked in a fire lit with embers from the kiln itself.

The different ages of the participants ensured that different generations exchanged memories, opinions and shared an experience that has to do with the ancient past through senses other than vision (Figure 2.5). This is an event still remembered in the village, and the different ways in which it resurfaces are manifold. It is either the memento kept by locals, baked clay statuettes or utensils, a reminiscence of the working of the clay for younger generations, the jokes exchanged

Figure 2.4 Mrs. Martha and Mrs. Eleni recreating their childhood clay toys. Photo by Aris Anagnostopoulos.

between young men on their creations, and so on and so forth. Most villagers were involved in one or another stage of this process, and in retrospect it seems like making and firing clay artifacts opened a new avenue of knowledge about the ancient past, one that is based on first-hand experience of the processes of creation. The actual experience of making and firing a clay figurine has added knowledge that cannot be conveyed otherwise. Looking through the narrow porthole of the kiln into an assemblage of clay items consumed by the fire that almost burns one's face but coming out unscathed, hardened, is a somatic experience that cannot be replaced by any visual aid or storytelling.

This experience has turned figurines and other clay artifacts into something that the community feels viscerally attached to, for they

Figure 2.5 Mr. Anastos digging up clay deposits with other participants at the workshop. Photo by Lena Stefanou.

constitute a part of their collective memory. They have stories to tell about how they participated in a workshop that made those figurines. They somewhat feel closer to the people they made them, not in any abstract ideological sense, but in a bodily way. The object biography for these remains of the ancient past has changed significantly. From bits of material that feel insignificant to them but may hide a greater value in centers of power and knowledge elsewhere, they become part of the communal experience and knowledge. This leads to them appreciating more the tiny bits of clay discovered in their fields and pasture lands, and feel that they ought to protect and preserve them for future generations.

References

Antoniadou, Ioanna. 2009. "Reflections on an Archaeological Ethnography of 'Looting' in Kozani, Greece." *Public Archaeology* 8 (2-3): 246–61.

Antoniadou, Ioanna. 2014. *Looting Deconstructed: A Study of Non-professional Engagements with the Material Past in Kozani, Greece.* Unpublished PhD Thesis, University of Southampton, Faculty of Humanities.

Appadurai, Arjun. 1986. "Introduction: Commodities and the Politics of Value." In *The Social Life of Things: Commodities in Cultural Perspective*, edited by Arjun Appadurai, 3–63. Cambridge: Cambridge University Press.

Damaskos, Dimitris, and Dimitris Plantzos (eds). 2008. *Singular Antiquity: Archaeology and Hellenic Identity in Twentieth-Century Greece.* Athens: Benaki Museum.

Deltsou, Eleftheria. 2009. "Researching Biographies of Archaeological Sites: The Case of Sikyon." *Public Archaeology* 8 (2–3): 176–90.

Duke, Phillip. 2007. *The Tourists Gaze, The Cretans Glance: Archaeology and Tourism on a Greek Island.* London: Routledge.

Gosden, Chris, and Marshall, Yvonne. 1999. "The Cultural Biography of Objects." *World Archaeology* 31 (2): 169–78.

Hamilakis, Yannis. 2007. *The Nation and Its Ruins: Antiquity, Archaeology, and National Imagination in Greece.* Oxford: Oxford University Press.

Hamilakis, Yannis. 2013. *Archaeology and the Senses. Human Experience, Memory, and Affect.* Cambridge: Cambridge University Press.

Hodder, Ian. 1982. *The Present Past. An Introduction to Anthropology for Archaeologists.* New York: Pika Press.

Holtorf, Cornelius. 2002. "Notes on the Life History of a Pot Sherd." *Journal of Material Culture* 7 (1): 49–71.

Joy, Jody. 2009. "Reinvigorating Object Biography: Reproducing the Drama of Object Lives." *World Archaeology* 41: 540–56.

Kyriakidis, Evangelos. 2005. Ritual in the Aegean: The Minoan Peak Sanctuaries, London:Duckworth

Murphy, Céline. 2020. "Ceramicists, Apprentices or Part-Timers? On the Modelling and Assembling of Peak Sanctuary Figurines." *EXARC Journal* 2020/3. https://exarc.net/ark:/88735/10518 (last accessed 10 December 2021).

Peatfield, Alan. 1990. "Minoan Peak Sanctuaries: History and Society." *Opuscula Atheniensia* XVIII (8): 117–31.

Peatfield, Alan. 2009. "The Topography of Minoan Peak Sanctuaries Revisited." *Hesperia Supplements* 42: 251–9.

Platon, Nikolaos. 1955. "Chronika." *Kritika Chronika* 9 (3): 517–69.

Scarpaci, Joseph. (2016). "Material Culture and the Meaning of Objects." *Material Culture* 48 (1): 1–9.

Solomon, Esther. 2006. "Knossos. Social Uses of a Monumental Landscape." *Creta Antica* 7: 163–82.

Trigger, Bruce. 1989. *A History of Archaeological Thought.* Cambridge: Cambridge University Press.

Witmore, Christopher. 2015. "Confronting Things." *Journal of Contemporary Archaeology* 1 (2): 239–46.

Yalouri, Eleana. 2001. *The Acropolis. Global Fame, Local Claim.* Oxford: Berg.

3 Negotiating walking routes to knowledge

A small place such as a village is deceptively local. It is, conversely, a node in a multiplicity of flows; of people, information, power and materials. The naturalized understanding of a village as a small, out-of-the way place is often put to the test by the expanse of this network of flows, both regionally and translocally. This spreading out happens in the context of the profound changes urbanization and out-migration has brought about for rural places in Greece and elsewhere. What this means for Gonies is a tremendous change in the way that landscape is understood and felt. A deep ethnographic exposition of this change is necessary as a base to understand our planning and development of a heritage path, which is described in the latter part of the chapter. It details the common decisions that led to our development of a path as a performative activity, rather than a material object, placed into the landscape in a final and unchanging way. Taking into consideration the local forms of landscape perception, the transformation of place memory through historical processes, as well as the pressures from tourism demand, we propose here a different option of heritage paths, not as demonstrable, material alterations to a landscape, but as activated knowledge communally owned by a local group.

Of roads, landscape and archaeology

Yannis, wearing a leather jacket with shoulders that look filled to capacity, is making his way uphill in a bitterly cold April morning. We struggle to keep up. He has driven us zooming down the road from the village in his four-wheel drive pickup-truck to a place north of the Gonies gorge known to locals as *Sorós*. He is grabbing the opportunity to show the archaeologists what he believes are ancient remains on the top of the steep hillside. He has taken state archaeologists on the same trip several times already to show them the paving stones

DOI: 10.4324/9781003259367-4

now under our feet. This is an old road, about two meters wide, paved in flat stones of various sides, made slippery from continuous use through the ages, exposure to the elements and the light drizzle that keeps falling around us. He jumps from wall to wall, pointing here, looking there, calling for one or another of us to come see something. He claims that the abandoned sheep pens we see around us are ancient buildings. We look at each other in exhausted disbelief.

Yannis has become over the years an 'expert' on tracing man-made constructions in the landscape. Talking to elders in the village, picking up place names and descriptions, but also walking or driving to almost anywhere on the surrounding area of Gonies, he is able to identify land formations that are not readily visible to even a well-trained archaeological eye. Many times he has shown us an almost imperceptible line on a mountain wall, lost in vegetation and looking like any other stone around it. It turns out it is a path, a wall, or a corner of a building. He has walked most of this area himself when little, taking supplies up to the mountains to his shepherd father and his collaborators, or leading the donkey loaded with firewood down the same path. In his four by four, there is always a round Styrofoam-lined flask of cold water and a *verga*, the crooked, thick wooden stick that shepherds use when walking in the mountains, or to catch disobeying animals, or to settle disputes with unruly neighbors.

Yannis insists that the archaeologists must come and excavate the area around Gonies. He is eager to show that the ancient Minoan road passed through Gonies, and not any other village in the area. We chat for a while, he is quite bitter that the archaeologists are so slow to respond despite the multiple strands of evidence of ancient settlements here. He punctuates his soliloquy with rhythmic waves of his hand, index finger and thumb put together as in an ok sign. Aris tries to humor him. What if we come here and excavate the whole area? What good will it do to the village? It will be destructive for the antiquities and invite the interest of looters. We cannot protect them after we expose them. Aris tries not sure he hears all this, looking down at his fingers, absentmindedly picking on a scab on the back of his hand. I don't know what you're telling me, he says in the end, I know what I told you.

Coming from an archaeological background, our research team is ready to listen to the persistent calls of locals to increase archaeological presence in the area. Based on success stories – real or imagined – of neighboring municipalities, archaeology is seen as a practical way, and a network of people, resources and power that can turn local knowledge into real improvements for this place. These improvements may pass through vague hopes for tourist development, but their ultimate aim is to regenerate the community itself, "to bring people back to the village" as Yannis, and other locals, put it. We need to pause here, for a second, however, to question how our own presence in the village, achieved through the usual networks of archaeological knowledge production and state-led preservation, in fact created a community of interest for archaeology. The point here is not just that our discipline allows us to see only the part of the picture that interests us but also something more tangible: that our own presence and activity in a place, combined with the historical experience of archaeology in the broader area and the widespread public images of archaeological treasures, is a machine that turns local knowledge into an archaeologically oriented pursuit of development. In simpler words, through our presence archaeology is seen as an opportunity to turn local knowledge and heritage into a profit-making and community-regenerating initiative, as we proposed (Kyriakidis 2019, 47). This initiative in turn influences the way locals and non-locals think about their place in terms of authenticity, temporality and material presence.

Landscape knowledge

But how, and most importantly *what,* does Yannis know? What sort of landscape knowledge does he carry and how does it connect to a collective memory of place? This sort of landscape knowledge is an aggregate of stories, places, traces, tidbits of information and placenames accumulated through everyday involvement in time with a place or with people associated with the place. The accumulation of such knowledge became evident to us in a guided tour given to Aris by Christos, a nearly centenarian shepherd. Driving in the car toward the plateau of Evdomos to the east of the village, Christos pointed at places and pronounced their names in an official-sounding manner; almost all places had a history to go with them. A dramatic incident, a strange occurrence, an uncommon cultivable, an arresting trait, were all anchors to a memory of place that unfolded like a palimpsest during our drive. One realizes, however, that the memory of a place or of places gets stronger by the repetitive overwriting of stories and histories, a repetition that in its turn is both spread out in time and also takes a lot of time to be recorded and recalled. Walking to a sheep pen high in the mountains would take quite some time; it would also follow a specific trajectory that changed only in very special occasions that should be nowadays even more memorable. Specific paths mean specific family allegiances, as different families kept their flocks in different parts of the mountain – and some still do. Specific paths also mean that the knowledge of places nearer or more visible from the path is stronger than that of places further away. This is a recognized fact in the village, and frequently, the landscape knowledge of even an elderly and respected shepherd will be judged on whether the place he is talking about was part of his pasture land, or was situated on the way to it. Conversely, elderly shepherds contest the landscape knowledge of younger ones, because they realize that the new modes of transport, pick-up trucks, cars or motorbikes, do not allow one to take the landscape in at the pace that walking or riding a donkey does. This resonates with what Ingold says about places that "do not have locations" (on maps)," but histories" (Ingold 2000, 229); place does not change only through movement into space but also through movement into time.

The topography of this place is the meeting ground for the distant and recent past, the present and, in some respects, the future (Basso 1996; Rappaport 1990, 9; Rosaldo 1980). The indexical nature of the landscape operates through representations in collective and personal memory to mediate the relationship, affective and cognitive, with its palpable, material register. This entanglement means that it is never a singular thing, but a plural patchwork of stories, memories and practices. Second, this meeting ground is very much a shifting ground as the social characteristics of the people living in the area change, and the function of landscape as indexical changes with it. The landscape itself is not a singular thing to be taken in, but an agglomeration of social practices and material potentialities. Nor is it a "traditional" body of knowledge, carried intact from generation to generation. It is rather a patchwork of knowledges, most of them disputed – intergenerationally, between families, between communities, between state and community, between people in conversation and so on (Kyriakidis 2019, 74). It also materializes a variety of temporal registers, when knowledge, symbols, names and practices from different times become inscribed and reinscribed on the same places, or places themselves lose their spatial specificity, acquired by use, and become indexical of larger areas. One such example is the dispute between the definitions offered by two representatives of two different generations of shepherds: a place known in the past as *Mavrogianniana* (meaning the area of the Mavrogiannis family, a name common in neighboring villages but not this one) was interpreted by a younger shepherd as *Mavrozoniana* (wearing a black belt). While the latter offered as proof of his knowledge that the place is within his turf, the area where his sheep graze, the older shepherd disputed this definition by offering as proof his own old age. According to him, it was called Mavrogianniáná as long as he can remember, and this is enough proof to discredit any other interpretation. But it is also a different register of temporality, where the life span of an older person is immediately understood as opening a door to the deep past – an assumption that we discuss further in the following chapter.

This landscape is not only the place of memory for a community of people, now dispersed globally, it is also a plural legal landscape shaped by a variety of authorities (cf. Anagnostopoulos 2021, 221). The control asserted onto this land has a variety of sources. One is the archaeological service that exercises its authority on antiquities, excavations and construction within archaeological zones of protection, or near places of archaeological interest. Simultaneously, there is the purview of the state and its tax authorities, that have only recently systematized their control over cultivable and pasture land, with the compilation of the land cadastre (*ktimatologio*). The solidification of knowledge about land, its whereabouts, its capacities, its ownership and its division into administrative areas around village communities, resulted in unexpected changes in the way that this land was perceived, owned and managed by communal authorities. In this case, a protracted legal battle took place between the community of Gonies and that of Anogeia to establish the borders between the two municipalities. Finally, this is land that is of great interest to energy-producing companies, that look at the seemingly abandoned pasture lands around the village as profitable investments and suitable lands to install solar panels and wind turbines, for a very small rent.

This landscape, furthermore, is a deeply gendered space. The mountains surrounding the village of Gonies constitute an "outside" space which has been considered, and still is, male territory, despite the fact that women also contributed daily to the cultivation of land. The memory and identity constructed around shepherd life creates a form of unruly masculinity that is not unique to this place, but its characteristics are very specific (Herzfeld 1985). The unruliness of Cretan men is thought to be an extension, if not a direct outcome, of the wilderness of Cretan mountains (Figure 3.1). The outside, the exterior, is deemed as more politically and morally superior place (Herzfeld 1985, 39). Concurrently, the inhabitants of the mountains are deemed more masculine, insubordinate, independent than their lowlands compatriots, who are perceived as more tame, submissive and sympathetic to state authority. This has an influence on the value hierarchies put on heritage – whereby activities associated with this exterior are more readily included in a notion of heritage worthy of preservation.

Figure 3.1 The annual shearing of sheep at the mountains near the village.
Photo by Aris Anagnostopoulos.

In the past decades, and even as these lines are being written, this landscape is changing perceptibly as the few permanent inhabitants of the village are passing away. From a lived and shifting environment of sociability, it is gradually transformed into a memory that needs to be preserved for the future generations: its importance as heritage becomes dominant. The affective power of such places is preserved in lexical indicators and toponyms: Yannis Markoyannakis, a Goniote civil engineer working in Iraklio admitted as much in a public workshop organized by the cultural association of the village in 2014: he confessed that he has written a long list of place-names from around the village and sometimes he will take the list out of his desk drawer and read it out loud to himself. The thrill of repeating those names stirs up powerful embodied feelings of nostalgia. Historical change thus transforms a lived environment into, as Foote notes, "a system of signs and symbols, capable of extending the temporal and spatial range of communication. In effect, the physical durability of landscape permits it to carry meaning into the future so as to help sustain memory and cultural traditions" (Foote 1997, 33).

It is evident that this nostalgia is exacerbated by the differential between the living memories of the inhabitants and the present state of the village. Mr. Anastos, a retired builder and poet has expressed this in spatial terms in one of his distichs:

"Από μακριά σα σε κοιτώ Γωνιές σε καμαρώνω./Μα στα στενά σου όταν μπω, κλαίω και δε μερώνω." [When I behold you from afar, Gonies, I feel proud/but when I walk your alleyways, I cry without end.]

(Athanasakis 2011)

In this honest and deeply moving distich, the temporal distance of an age of growth and hope and its contrast with the present state of the village is coupled with the spatial distance from it, and both are connected by vision. It is a testimony to the ways that nostalgia for the past is vectored both by temporal and spatial distance, for historical reasons that are inscribed in the memory of place.

These dialectics of seeing, which is a dialectics of distance, is much more embedded in the ontological patterns of Goniotes than one may first be led to believe. Our own training of the senses may initially prevent us to see just how mobile this seemingly sedate village is. Heritage, history and tradition have taught us to see villages as far-away places, isolated, compact and autonomous entities. The closer we look at the village however, the clearer it is that this is a node in a much larger network of movement of people and goods that has a remarkable historical depth. We can look at further aspects of this process of "heritagization," of the willing or unwitting transformation of lived places into sedentary, unmoving heritage landscapes or communication forms, usually geared toward tourist development (Foote 1997, 33; Walsh 1992, 138). But for the purposes of this chapter, it serves well to look at the ways archaeology as a form of "dwelling" (Ingold 2000, 189–90) has shaped this sense of landscape. Archaeological knowledge, shared among locals, those still in the village, in nearby Heraklio, or thousands of miles away, has changed the perception of the place, by adding to it a layer of deep time. At the same time, however, it also opened an avenue of potential development and profit through the spectral promises of mass tourism and its assimilation of archaeological and more recent heritage.

The Minoan road: from history and myth to regional politics

In the years leading to the second decade of the twenty-first century, several local developments that bring together archaeology, tourism, rural development, and the heritagization of the past and the natural environment took place in the mountainous areas of central Crete. Two large rural municipalities adjacent to Gonies, Krousonas and Anogeia, decided to draw funds from European Union programs to chart and pave their own 'Minoan Paths' to the top of mount Psiloritis. The idea behind these paths was that these were the original trajectories of king Minos and his retinue to the top of the mountain in Minoan times. The motivation was to attract more eco-friendly forms of tourism, that were more suited to rural mountainous areas. Seeing that the main volume of tourists to Crete gather at the seafronts of the North, in large resorts with all-inclusive packages, municipalities in the mainland of the island are slowly turning to forms of tourism like walking tourism and ecotourism.

The 'Minoan Path' however, has an additional function, as it solidifies and strengthens a sense of local pride for the municipalities involved. To vie for the privilege of being the place where king Minos passed on his way to renew his kingly mandate from Zeus, is to establish a place in the history of the island. At the same time, to be so securely tied to the most ancient form of civilization on the island, is to establish that these municipalities as more ancient, or, to put it more simply, "were there first." In the creation of 'Minoan paths', rural communities muster the, sometimes uninformed, opinions of various archaeologists to produce material and tangible "proofs" of their early presence in the area, and gain in moral superiority to neighboring communities. Zeus is perceived as the supreme ruler of a near-monotheistic religious system, and furthermore as a legendary personality that inhabited the very mountains where modern day shepherds dwell. In several of his modern incarnations in local art and music, Zeus is presented as a taciturn shepherd, living alone in the mountains of central Crete. The paths that 'Minos took' are some of the very paths that shepherds have been taking to their pastures for the last couple of centuries at least. They are also part of a very current social and cultural landscape as it is currently transformed by the powers of urbanization, modernization and heritagization.

It comes as no surprise then that the main avenue marking the Goniote approach to the past is "the Minoan road" (Markoyannakis 2011) (Figure 3.2 and Figure 3.3). The old paved road that Yannis was showing us on that drizzly April day and has shown us again and again in the following years, is to his eyes and those of many in the village, none other than the path king Minos would take every nine years to the top of Psiloritis mountain, to confer with his father, Zeus and renew his mandate. The first mention of such a route taken by Minos, the king of Crete, is in Plato *Laws* 624a-625c. In this largely fictional account based on

Homeric lore, Clinias, a Cretan, discusses with an unnamed Athenian the Cretan belief that king Minos renews his mandate every nine years in conversation with Zeus, his father, on top of mount Ida. Plato describes a long but comfortable journey under the shades of tall trees lining the road, and groves of cypress-trees "of wonderful height and beauty" further uphill (Plato 1926, 5).

Besides the hermeneutic approaches that would transform the cultural content of the landscape, and, if finally appended to local development schemes, would also reshape the material aspects of the environment, there is an economic consideration to this insistence. If the neighboring municipalities succeed in establishing the "real" 'Minoan path' in their turf, then, according to some locals, Gonies

Figure 3.2 Remains of a stone-paved road in the valley north of the village.

Figure 3.3 Charting out the old road, guided by locals. Photo by Lena
        Stefanou.

will be completely bypassed by the expected swarm of tourists that
will flood the area with their riches and a perceivably huge opportunity for local development will be lost. As we discuss below, however,
this expectation produces ambivalent feelings to locals. Roads and
accessibility, coupled with economic prosperity, are not only material
things, but also deeply embedded in memories of collective life, and
associated with the economic booms and busts that transformed the
experience of community life (cf. Dalakoglou 2010, 144).

The old road

We stand on the old stone-paved street, right in front of the disused
water mill, looking up at Philiorimos, its name evoking this sense of
desertion, *-erimos* meaning desolate (Kyriakidis 2018, 147). Sparse
noises are to be heard, and few people are visible outside. The tran-
quility is such, one is led to believe that this has always been a quiet
place. Fixed and immobile. Vassilis, a lively shepherd in his late eight-
ies, remembers otherwise. He points at the old stone-paved street, the
same street that Marinatos saw from the Minoan "villa" he excavated
in 1935, and exclaims:

This was an avenue!

An avenue?
Yes! Thousands of people! I would walk to my sheep shed and greet people all the way. People! If you told me today, I also would not believe it. But I believe it, because I saw it with my own eyes.

Where were these people going?
Everywhere. The city. Their fields. People! Most of them barefoot, you hear me? They would walk barefoot to the fields in the valley, their axes on their shoulders, some bread in their sack and that was all. Looking for work. Poor people. People and donkeys – I beg your pardon. They would go to the city with firewood, sell it and buy flour. A day's trip. Eh!

He waves his hand as if shooing the past back to its proper place. To believe that this road was bustling with people is hard. We are standing at a crossroads, in the middle of it, and yet we are not disturbed but by the occasional cicada, or a passing car at a distance. And yet he insists, even later at the *kafeneio* (coffee-shop), when he slams his arthritic-riddled hand on the table for emphasis. "This was a thousand-strong village. The school had three hundred children. Look at us now." This is the way locals tell their story; it is a story of decline. The village was once on its way to become a big, healthy, important place. Now, it is a small village of elderly people. What happened in the meantime?

Following materials and people as they move through space often uncovers a history much more mobile than previously expected. Philiorimos is one of the main sources of serpentinite – a hard, marble-like green stone – in eastern Crete. Many artifacts from serpentinite discovered in Knossos and elsewhere were probably made of stone from this particular area. This makes archaeologists suppose a well-developed trade in materials within the vicinity of Gonies in Minoan times. It is certain that this place was not as deserted as it looks today. Similarly, clay idols found on top of Philioremos were probably made from clay collected in the area. Some sources already located are within a range of one or two kilometers from the peak sanctuary where they were deposited. Even if current views on the construction of figurines far away are now challenged, it is probable that there was movement of specific materials to construct them on the spot.

In long expanses of their history, people in the area did not only carry material but also technical knowledge. Modern stonemasons point at a specific layout for stone walls in the village, which is called *scarpathiotiko*. It is named so because itinerant builders from Scarpathos, modern day Karpathos, came to the village and showed them how to build in this particular way. In fact, they insist that before the Scarpathiotes came to the village, locals did not know much about stonemasonry. Some place this visit at some point immediately before the World War II, while others insist that it was way further in the past. The connections of Crete with Karpathos are very much older. In Venetian, fourteenth-century Crete, the noble family of Corner, who owned large areas in Gonies, also owned shares in the island of Karpathos (McKee 2000, 64). While it is not certain that builders from that island came to Gonies during Venetian times, this information is indicative of connections that may have existed between these two islands, seen as part of a common dominion. Goniotes themselves took up the trade of the itinerant stonemason especially after WWII, gradually beginning to make a name for themselves throughout the island.

Itinerant life was not strange to most inhabitants of the village. Shepherds often formed companies (*patoulies*) to lead their sheep over huge distances to warmer seaside pastures in the winter and bring them back during the summer. One family, for example, and their herding partners used to take their sheep on foot all the way to the Malia plain, some sixty kilometers to the east in early winter. They would stay there until April, and then return on foot again to the mountains of Gonies. In a similar way, in the early 1970s, a group of itinerant stonemasons, mostly from another village family, united to go to Malia and build the bungalows of a large hotel there. They stayed in place as long as the building demanded. They were used to sleeping rough, spending time away from home and family. It was a manly thing to do, they had learned so in their village, and digested it better while doing their civil service in the Greek army. A minimum of three years' service away from friends and family was the norm up until the 1980s in Greece, and these young men were expected to live up to the experience. How could they not to, when their whole life was not the sedentary life traditionally associated with rural places, but a highly mobile regime dictated by need.

Displacement and mobility in the creation of local identity

Even today, it is difficult to place Gonies. The sense of locality is strong: a writer from Gonies, nowadays living in northern Greece, has named it *gonianosyni* – goniesness (Papadakis 2001). But this sense of being from this place is rather exaggerated by the high mobility of its people. Widespread understanding of villages as small, local places, prevent us from seeing the expanse that these villages sometimes have in space, or their mobility through time. A significant part of the activity of Gonies happens in the northeastern axis, on the road that connects this village with the seaside settlement of Gazi. This one-time marshland is a flat seaside expanse of land watered by the confluence of small rivulets from the mountains on its south. Chourmouzis, writing a geography of Crete in 1842, has this much to say of this place and its adjacent villages: "Gazi and Kavrochori, villages full of disease" (Chourmouzis 1842, 46).

Out-migration from the village led to resettlement of many families in the Gazi area, where land was cheap and readily available. So it is now natural for many families to have a house in or near Gazi, where the newer generation of Goniotes lives, and a house in the village, where the elderly spend their time. Many younger Goniotes spend a lot of time driving up to the village, often spend a night or two there or return overnight. They bring provisions, visit their families, run errands or take people to state services in Gazi or Heraklio. The administrative seat of the municipality of Malevizi is in Gazi. Villagers have to go there to register for services. It is natural for a younger Goniote to drive the road to Heraklio and back three or four times a week.

For a project like ours that seeks to be engaged in community regeneration in the village, the question of locality arises continuously (Kyriakidis 2019, 44–5). But this is a question that Goniotes themselves pose, fully aware of the tensions arising from a dispersal of the village in post-war history. The village "group" is no longer territorialized, bound in space. It is no longer aware of its own history, or, despite pronouncements to the contrary, partaking to a common "culture." This is a characteristic shared with many other localities in the global landscapes of group identity, or "ethnoscapes" (Appadurai 1991, 191).

However much this dispersal is felt in the life of the village itself, it is nevertheless neither a modern feature nor a straightforward one. As we have already described above, the place was always marked by very high seasonal mobility and migration of families and populations. But what is more crucial in our context is that the more a community becomes deterritorialized, the more it arises as a strong signifier that brings people together in global ethnoscapes. New technologies, instead of creating a more global consciousness, have actually been used to strengthen already established spatial belonging. When we first created the Three Peak Sanctuary Facebook page, we included a short description on the page profile.[1] In the description, we identified the three peak sanctuaries with their established name in archaeological nomenclature. One of them, Keria, was investigated by the archaeologist Antonis Vasilakis. Since Vasilakis reached Keria from the neighboring village of Krousonas, he named it Keria Krousonas in all ensuing references. And this is how we named it on our profile description in the evening that this page was made. The next morning, Aris received an anxious call from the president of the Cultural Association of the village. He talked in stern concentration. He asked: "how is Keria known in the scientific nomenclature? As Keria Krousonas? Because if so, it is plainly wrong." "Keria belongs to Gonies," he said, "and the village has papers to prove it." It turned out that the phrasing was spotted by Goniote immigrants in the US, who promptly reported it to the cultural association.

The extension of the notion of community creates connected networks of information that span a space much larger than the village or its regional vicinity and are mediated by a variety of media. Representations of the village exist in YouTube channels, Facebook groups and profiles, Google maps, Instagram photos and a variety of other pages. This is also a place where the village exists, or a notion of community, to be more precise, creating a much different sense of landscape. This sense of landscape is very much connected to a nostalgic memory of the pastoral ways of the past. It is not so much an inhabited landscape, a space that can be taken in on foot or surveyed from a high vantage point, but a shared memoryscape, which is enhanced by repeat visits to the actual place.

For all the public character of these representations, there is a very pronounced sense of ownership of images, names and knowledge. Strangely, this sense of ownership aims to prevent items from this memoryscape from "spilling out" of the confines of the village proper. During our 2014 season in the village, we wanted to do a photographic art installation (see previous chapter), using the photographic archive of the village cultural association, which we were digitizing at the time. It turned out that using the photographs, donated by villagers to the cultural association for the purpose of setting up a photo album of documents from the past life of the village, was a very complicated process. We heard of concerns that we were going to take photographs away from the village and exhibit them elsewhere, without the explicit permission of people pictured in them. We had to explain in a long and laborious effort of mediation that this was never our intention, and show all proposed installation material to the concerned parties before it was possible to happen.

Identifying the road as a symbol

Faced with the wild dispersion of people, objects, images and interpretations, the road to the village – in its subsequent materializations through time – becomes a symbolic index of the perceived lost core of community cohesion. Despite the resilience of "gonianosyni," despite the familial bonds that hold people over distance even in this dispersed context, the view from the village is one of abandonment, and not resilience. And indeed, staying there in the winter is an experience of solitude, destitution and distance from the center of national life and progress.

Looking back at the processes that dispersed an otherwise thriving community from this vantage point, however, occludes the fact that most of the people who left the village did so in search for a better life. For many, the improvement in their quality of life was very palpable. The nostalgia for the lost community disguises this fact for both 'experts' and 'non-experts'. Contrary to what Herzfeld noted for the villagers of Glendi, the memory narrated here is not one of poverty, nor do such discourses come up as excuses for animal theft in the past (Herzfeld 1985, 164). The stories told in Gonies are stories of a booming community, thriving in numbers and living a good life. Yet, the cramped, tiny remains of village houses point to a much different story, of a community cramped to capacity, making do with sparse resources and intensive cultivation and animal husbandry. The fields are just as cramped as the houses, every nook and cranny amidst sharp rocks put to cultivation.

This transition to a better life is visible in the makeup of the village. Mrs. Eleni took us on a walk to the house where she was born and raised. She opened the door, the two wooden halves rotten by the wind and rain, latched with a piece of wire. The two adjacent rooms are so narrow you can almost reach the walls with your hands outstretched. She showed us the interior; seven children, two parents, several animals – donkey, goats, rabbits, chicken – shared the same space, which was simultaneously kitchen, bedroom, workspace for the loom of the house, playroom for the children. Animals, people and objects fit in an almost ergonomic arrangement. Humans slept on elevated platforms reached by a ladder, the children in one room and the parents in the other. The donkey was parked under the parents' bed, the rabbit coop under the children's. The single, tiny barred window allowed a slither of light to come in. Fewer windows meant better insulation against the cold in winter, but permanent damp during the year also. We walked outside with a sense of relief, while Mrs. Eleni pointed to the second floor of the house, visibly constructed much later by her father, with a sense of pride. This pride was not unwarranted, since this testified to the family's prosperity and advancement in life. Compared to the houses she showed us next door, single-room constructions leaning against each other, in which it was difficult to understand how even a single person dwelled, this was indeed a luxurious abode.

Newer houses, built more spacious and usually detached from older ones, were signs of the improvement after the WWII. Significantly, they were also material signs of the dissolution of the older bonds that held the village together. In the past, houses were constructed in tight nuclei, primarily out of need; sturdy existing walls diminished building cost and saved material; land was sparse, and family ownership was divided to heirs, parceled out in ever diminishing pieces of land. The expectation that the first son, or the most able one, would branch out and make his own house was there, but the dire necessities of life almost always made this rule an exception. After the war, materials were cheaper, and access to technical innovations like reinforced concrete opened new areas up for building. This geographical spread was coterminous with the gradual dissolution of the tight nucleus of the neighborhood as a core of livelihood and sociability, as a built space for communal bonds, shared conviviality and social control. The shared space of the village changed its character. What is now remembered as the old square of the village, in *archontika*, was until the early twentieth century a chain of rooftops from adjacent houses, that was used for gatherings in festive occasions. Those houses, abandoned in time, were then demolished to make space for an opening that resembles more a square as we are used to understand it.

The demand for close coexistence and community help was replaced by the demand for greater access. In the past, the close coexistence of people was also dictated by their everyday needs. Simple tasks, like acquiring bread, were communally managed. Women would knead dough and make breads which they would later take to the wood oven owned by a neighborhood household. Wood ovens were not rare but were sparse and wide apart. The women who owned them would bake the bread of a group of families, usually living nearby, and charge a loaf for each batch. With the transformation of the village and out-migration, these tasks were progressively relegated to outsiders. First, a bakery was made in the village that sold bread to those who had lost access to an oven. Later, as wood ovens became a rare occurrence, and the village became depopulated, the bakery was replaced by an itinerant seller of bread that arrives every day to the village to sell his produce. This transformation made access a significant demand of the village inhabitants: access to services and goods is imperative for them, who depend on outside sources for their subsistence and survival. So, the condition of roads becomes a central concern to the locals. But, at the same time, the increased prosperity of migrants to the city, and their seasonal transition to the village, create demands that change the character of access to holiday luxury: a retired military officer with a house in the *archontika* has been lobbying local authorities for quite a while now to demolish the remains of houses on the top of the old village to make way for a road accessible to cars. His rationale is simple, that this road will allow better access by car to the core of the old village, and thus make it more attractive to holiday makers and seasonal returnees. People will have a place to park their cars. This developmental rationale meets with reactions from more heritage-minded people but is significant to show how an understanding of roads as access transforms itself and influences heritage conservation.

While heritage understandings may lead us to conceptualize space and place as a fixed entity, the nature of this knowledge is in fact deeply kinetic. Even in this era, where most of the village inhabitants are sedentary due to old age, technological advancements have ensured that the village itself and its surrounding are never the small place, outside the flows of information, value and goods that pastoral fantasies may have it to be. It is deeply embedded in networks of movement and exchange.

An aspect of landscape knowledge in Gonies has certainly become inert heritage precisely because it got disconnected from an everyday practice. It is in dire need of preservation precisely because it has become practically obsolete. But at the same time, there is another aspect of this knowledge that is at the core of the resilience of its inhabitants. This process, whereby local knowledge becomes exclusively "intangible" heritage through the obsolescence of older means of production and older forms of social organization, intersects with much larger-scale processes of urbanization, modernization, and the commodification of local ways of life through regional development, tourist or otherwise. When we begin planning a collaborative way of addressing this transformation, we realized that there are different perspectives on future development, different political or micropolitical views, that need to be addressed, discussed or answered in the preservation and management of heritage.

From learning about to learning with

How can this knowledge about landscape, intermixed as it is with new developments in roads and transportation, and the symbolic import of development and archaeology, taken in the context of history and heritage, come to be known in any significant way by a team of heritage 'experts' working with the village community? How can these efforts provide alternative narratives that are inclusive of many voices within a community? And how can these be connected with a process of sustainable development?

We had all these considerations in mind when we set out to create a heritage path in the village. There is a strong tendency in current social research away from representational modes of ethnographic research, toward more performative actions in the field (e.g. Hamilakis and Theou 2013; Tolia-Kelly 2007). These actions put greater emphasis in the affective load of spaces and their embodied perception. They also put a heavier stress on the evocative aspects of memory spaces, rather on the cognitive content that 'experts' may put into them. In this context, walking in heritage trails may prove a surprisingly simple, but effective technique that brings ethnomethodological considerations together with techniques that evoke the phenomenological aspects of place as they emerge (O'Neill and Hubbard 2010, 47). Indeed, Ingold and Vergunst point to the fact that walking is not a habitual activity, but instead a way to think and feel that continuously generates cultural forms (2008, 2).

Given our limited resources, both ours as a project and of the community itself, we thought that a heritage path would function at many levels: first of all, it would be a form of collectively creating knowledge about the place, by using the same performative means through which this knowledge is carried. A combination of immersive ethnographic research, community engagement and artistic practice pointed directly to the value of mimetic performances as embodied ways of sensuous knowledge (O'Neill and Hubbard 2010, 48). As is obvious from this chapter, what is known about this landscape is a multilayered combination of practices, movements, paths, institutions, texts, stories and processes, that cannot solely be conveyed in textual forms. An ethnomimetic process (O'Neill et al. 2002) through art practice enables us, in collaboration with the community, to make these multiple layers felt in the context where they emerge.

Second, the means of giving out this information to the public would be along the same experiential lines, and not as a separate exhibition of the place. It would also eventually serve as a method of engagement of locals in the process of sharing their knowledge. Third, we realized in consultation with tour guides of the area, that this could be a good way to bring more visitors to the village, by creating an information pack that could attract self-guided tourists to the area.

It was our aim from the beginning to show how the heritage of the village could be promoted by using simple means that require minimal funds. At the same time, we wanted to highlight the fact that memories, stories, practices and places in the village could have significance for people outside it. It was important to show to the current inhabitants that there is potential to the village developing a visitor base, and that no big development is necessary for that. To do this, we wanted to safeguard two things: first, that we would construct an archive of activities, something like a toolkit that the community could pick up in the future and use for itself, without our presence there. While it was strange to give walking tours of the village to locals and descendants of local families, it was nevertheless necessary to familiarize locals with what was expected by visitors, and make them understand that this is feasible within the limited means of the community. We did these things more to set an example, present a case where local knowledge would creatively become something to be shared with visitors and interested groups.

During the first year of the Summer School, in 2014, the archaeologist and visual artist Vasko Demou collaborated with us to set up an open-air art exhibition based on the ethnographic information already created in the village. We wanted to devise an affordable, accessible and aesthetically inclusive way to give this information back to locals, but also to share it with visitors. The installations were simple drawings or cardboard frames with information from a variety of sources. Some were drawn from the rich photographic community archive that we digitized that same year. Others were texts drawn from archaeological publications on Gonies, or oral recitations given to us by locals. Yet others were representations of larger bodies of information or processes that we wanted to highlight – for example, we drew footsteps on the road surface representing the women queueing up for water at the village spring (Figure 3.4).

The unifying rationale for this exhibition was the creation of a path in the village that would bring visitors to successive steps of the exhibition. We came to this decision by looking at how the locals themselves thought and remembered the place, as was described above. Throughout our research with the village, a number of people have offered to take us on a walking tour of the village, to show us the house where they grew up, or their old neighborhood. It was a first approximation of the performative way in which locals remembered their own place. At the same time, however, it tried to create a path through the village that was easily manageable by a visitor on foot, as well as inclusive of the many narratives we heard during our research in the village. Instead of drawing a specific route, using for example numbered steps in a process through the village, we opted for a more open form, in

Figure 3.4 Women's prints reproduced on the road surface. Photo by Lena
    Stefanou.

which the path is drawn following an abstract map of the village. By
doing this, we avoided ranking places in order of importance, something that brought some interesting reactions (Figure 3.5).

The main criticism this map received was on a gender basis: older
men felt that it did not represent the full importance of the history of
the village, as it included aspects of everyday life in the past that were
explicitly female, for example neighborhood wood ovens, or narratives
that were female in their importance, such as legends about the *lygaria*
(chaste tree) and songs about the virgin Mary. These aspects, furthermore, were presented on the same page with what is considered a more
masculine aspect of heritage, heroic feats by ancestors of the families

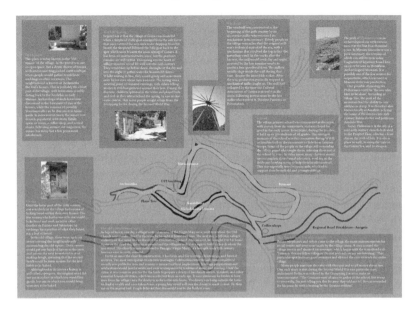

Figure 3.5 A collectively drawn heritage map of the village.

now living in the village. The coexistence of male and female spaces on the map opened up a space for the discussion on what exactly should be included in a local definition of heritage.

This resistance to alternative narratives about heritage, or even the multiplicity of such, must be considered by heritage 'experts' in the creation of similar programs. We were in the paradoxical position of having to defend aspects of the memory of the place against interpretations that came from within the community and obviously sustained power relations within it. But at the same time, we realized that our map was not the heritage of the village, just another interpretation of it, despite the fact that we aimed to be as inclusive as possible. At this early stage of public collaborative action, we realized that if we wanted to facilitate the discussion on the creation and preservation of heritage, our role should be limited to creating social spaces to accommodate it. Our efforts in this direction are described in further detail in the next chapter.

Creating these installations in the village aimed to give back the information gained through ethnographic research in an accessible form, and create novel ethnographic encounters. But at the same time, these installations had the additional function of serving as performative acts that highlighted specific material aspects of the village as heritage worthy of mention and preservation. During the preparations for the exhibition, when the footsteps were drawn near the old spring of the village, a woman approached Lena Stefanou and quizzed her on the action. Lena started describing to her in what she and the students were doing: she described how they were trying to depict the standing in queue of the village women, waiting to fill their earthenware pots with water. The woman seemed to have none of it, reacting to this gratuitous and seemingly pointless soiling of the road surface. At which point, Lena switched her linguistic register and started using the expressions used by village women to describe this act: she said that women were waiting *mè to nobèti* (in queue) to fetch water. Her interlocutor's face lit up and, overjoyed, she went on to thank her for doing all this to preserve the old ways of life and for paying such attention to otherwise inconsequential everyday acts.

The process of drawing a heritage path in the village was therefore for us a first step in engaging the community. But this we later understood in retrospect. What we understood particularly was that, instead of us preparing a ready-made action which we then applied on the village and expected the villagers to engage in it, we instead took several smaller steps which progressively involved more and more people in shaping, directing, and offering material for public presentations. This is a lesson that archaeological ethnography can offer to heritage management specialists: the time necessary to develop a heritage scheme is of importance, not only for the creation of knowledge and the establishment of trust. Time is also a more integral element to the development of relations of cooperation, in setting up increasing levels of engagement.

In the following years, while the summer school developed and grew in recognition within the village, we collectively decided to expand this path-making in the areas that surround the village. In 2015, the ethnographic work of students in the village was again turned into an archive-making exercise where knowledge created with the village was recorded and returned to the community in easily accessible written form, or other verbal and non-verbal ways of expression.

When Mrs. Eleni, for example, gave us an extensive walking tour of the part of the village she grew up in and showed us her family house during the 2015 summer school, the marked difference in this very recent and very close-to-home way of life profoundly struck our students – and us. The radical alterity of this way of life, located furthermore so close to shared assumptions of progress and "civilized" manners, made this a difficult subject to breach and present to a visiting public. While the poverty and deprivation of the village in the past is something that is barely hidden, there is a certain ambivalence in the way this poverty as a way of life and motivating force is approached. Local pride and the narrative of village decline present it as a thriving and strong village. On the other hand, there emerge moments in this narrative that emphasize the deprivation that led people out of the village and into the cities, but also a scathing critique of past ways of life, that is usually expressed in humorous terms (see Herzfeld 1985, 164–5). However, as Herzfeld himself has also noted, the complexities of cultural intimacy may have been problematic in any straight-forward description of these ways of life. To put it otherwise, any verbatim transfer of descriptions of poverty would have resulted in reactions and concerns. While locals may gladly share stories about the hardships of everyday life, they are very guarded against these stories spreading outside the village. These memories are very strong, but given the local understanding of the hierarchies of value associated with town and country, urbanite and villager, developed and backward. Instead of using verbal cues to describe the living arrangements of this family, that were common throughout the village, we opted for another, matter-of-fact form of description. Based on Mrs. Eleni's description, we produced a plan of her family house, with people and animals in the areas she indicated, that references similar archaeological floor plans of older abodes, in a more simplified visual manner (Figure 3.6). Mrs Eleni approved of this form of presentation and found it incredibly accurate: "this is exactly how it was," she said, and thanked us and enthusiastically thanked us for representing "our ways of life."

In the second and third year of the summer school (2015–2016), we tried to expand the visitor basis for the final presentation of research work and also invite tour guides who develop cultural tourism packages to showcase our work in the village and perhaps work together to make it a destination of those tours. This expansion of the visitor basis slowly started shaping the presence of locals in these events into a more active participation. This is the first year that we realized that these touring events had another aspect in the preservation and shaping of local heritage. Our presentations began to be more and more populated by second- and third-generation Goniotes who live in the city of Heraklio, but also from abroad. In view of the dispersal of the village community, our efforts at highlighting the tangible and intangible heritage of the village gradually became an educational process for the passing of knowledge to later generations that did not reside in the village. While we were still focused in creating a concise and interesting heritage path for potential visitors from outside, we began

Figure 3.6 A plan of the living arrangements of an old house, displayed outside its front door. Photo: Lena Stefanou.

to realize that paths like this have a multiple character, and are not
simply visitor-oriented attractions, but may become an open archive
for local history and heritage.

It was during this process, and our consultation with tour guides
and agencies that organized walking tours that we realized that
this form of tourism has specific characteristics that shape the way
we understand landscape in general. On the one hand, the aesthetic
aspect of these walks remains strong. As attractions, tourist paths in
landscapes like Crete still sell based on the "wild beauty" of the Cretan
landscape developed in printed tourist guides addressed mainly to a
middle-class audience. To understand this aesthetic value as a natural
occurrence is to see only half of the story, since what is perceived as
the ruggedness of Cretan scenery is in fact produced and reproduced
through a variety of media, agencies and processes. In our case, while
the landscape of Gonies has great value and significance for locals
and people associated with them, it lacks the picturesque sights and
tourist-friendly routes that turn other areas in Crete into mainstays of
alternative forms of tourism.

This leads to a paradox whereby potentially benign forms of tourism do, in the long run, form a hierarchy of value for places and sites; it also runs the risk of valuating the landscape experience of a place as a product, and managing it accordingly. An option proposed by some tour guides was to create and experience-rich heritage path along the lines that we had already began doing. What we understood, however, is that the formation of such a path has different considerations and priorities than we would expect as engaged researchers, thinking from the village outward: for example, the length of such a path has to be sufficiently large for a visitor to be worth her while, but not too large as to require dedication to complete, or to compete with a busy schedule of visits.

Simultaneously, however, the way that such tour operators work may provide an adequate framework for forging links between the local place making and open archive process and the more eco-friendly and community-friendly aspects of the tourist industry. Local offices that organize walking tours usually do not give the tours themselves, but collect and provide material that allows visitors to choose a route that suits their needs, preferences and time. This meant that we did not need to "open" a path, mark it and perhaps give it a material form, such as a paved surface etc., as is usually the case of state or EU-sponsored heritage paths in Crete or elsewhere. On the contrary, this allowed us to attune the resources of the village and its performative understanding of landscape to forms of visit that were more inclusive and open to the society itself. At the same time, it meant that we could look to a platform that would support the practical aspects of our work, besides academic publications such as this book, and it would achieve an outreach beyond the confines of the local.

As may have been obvious from the above, we did not conceptualize a path as something that we would complete and then make available to an interested public, but as an ongoing process of creating and curating knowledge, forging bonds, and safeguarding the integrity of landscape and local knowledge. Our concept of the path was based precisely on a concept of co-curation. A path in this case is not a material unity, but an agglomeration of points, bits of knowledge, stories, interesting places, place-names. An assortment of heritage elements that cannot be dissociated from the people who carry them, and who have a strong part in conveying it and turning it once again into active knowledge. The path is there, in leaflets we have coproduced with locals, in maps that are available to visitors in the village, but, perhaps more importantly, as activated knowledge that can lead to encounters and cross-cultural meetings between interested visitors and locals.

Note

1. See https://www.facebook.com/ThreePeakSanctuariesProject/

References

Anagnostopoulos, Aris. 2021. "Archaeological 'Protection Zones' and the Limits of the Possible. Archaeological Law, Abandonment and Contested Spaces in Greece." In: Esther Solomon (ed.), *Contested Antiquity: Archaeological Heritage and Social Conflict in Modern Greece and Cyprus*. Bloomington: University of Indiana Press.

Appadurai, Arjun. 1991. "Global Ethnoscapes: Notes and Queries for a Transnational Anthropology." In: Richard Gabriel Fox (ed.), *Recapturing Anthropology: Working in the Present*. Santa Fe, New Mexico: School of American Research Press, 48–65.

Athanasakis, Anastos. 2011. *Sta Monopathia tsi Zois* [In the paths of life]. Heraklion: n.p.

Basso, Keith H. 1996. *Wisdom Sits in Places: Landscape and Language among the Western Apache*. Albuquerque: University of New Mexico Press.

Chourmouzis, Byzantios. 1842. *Kritika*. Athens: Agathi Tychi Press.

Dalakoglou, Dimitris. 2010. "The Road: An Ethnography of the Albanian–Greek Cross-Border Motorway." *American Ethnologist* 37: 132–149.

Foote, Kenneth. 1997. *Shadowed Ground: America's Landscapes of Violence and Tragedy*. Austin: University of Texas Press.

Hamilakis, Yannis and Efthimis Theou. 2013. "Enacted Multi-Temporality: The Archaeological Site as a Shared, Performative Space." In Alfredo González Ruibal (ed.), *Reclaiming Archaeology: Beyond the Tropes of Modernity*. London: Routledge, 181–195.

Herzfeld, Michael. 1985. *The Poetics of Manhood. Contest and Identity in a Cretan Mountain Village*. Princeton: Princeton University Press.

Ingold, Tim. 2000. *The Perception of the Environment. Essays on Livelihood, Dwelling and Skill*. London: Routledge.

Ingold, Tim, and Jo Lee Vergunst. 2008. *Ways of Walking: Ethnography and Practice on Foot*. Aldershot: Ashgate.

Kyriakidis, Evangelos. 2018. "The Onomatology of Philioremos, A Minoan Peak Sanctuary in Central Northern Crete." In: Giorgia Baldacci and Ilaria Caloi (eds.), *Rhadamanthys, BAR S2884*. Oxford: BAR Publishing.

Kyriakidis, Evangelos. 2019. *A Community Empowerment Approach to Heritage Management: From Values Assessment to Local Engagement*. London: Routledge.

Markoyannakis, Giorgos. 2011. "To taksidi tou Minoa sto Idaion Antro." *Patris Newspaper* 12.

McKee, Sally. 2000. *Uncommon Dominion. Venetian Crete and the Myth of Ethnic Purity*. Philadelphia: University of Pennsylvania Press.

O'Neill, Maggie and Phil Hubbard. 2010. "Walking, Sensing, Belonging: Ethno-Mimesis as Performative Praxis." *Visual Studies* 25 (1): 46–58.

O'Neill, Maggie, in association with Sarah Giddens, Patricia Breatnach, Carl Bagley, Darren Bourne, and Tony Judge. 2002. "Renewed Methodologies for Social Research: Ethno-Mimesis as Performative Praxis." *Sociological Review* 50 (1): 69–88.

Papadakis, Manolis. 2001. *Gonies. Ena taksidi sto chrono kai sto choro.* Thessaloniki: Ekdoseis Aplatanos.

Plato. 1926. *Laws, Volume I: Books 1-6.* Translated by R.G. Bury. Loeb Classical Library 187. Cambridge, MA: Harvard University Press.

Rappaport, Joanne. 1990. *The Politics of Memory: Native Historical Interpretations in the Colombian Andes.* Cambridge: Cambridge University Press.

Rosaldo, Renato. 1980. *Ilongot Headhunting: 1883–1974: A Study in History and Society.* Stanford: Stanford University Press.

Tolia-Kelly, Divya P. 2007. "Fear in Paradise: The Affective Registers of the English Lake District Re-visited." *Senses and Society* 2 (3): 329–52.

Walsh, Kevin. 1992. *The Representation of the Past. Museums and Heritage in the Postmodern World.* London: Routledge.

4   History and memory

Performative practices in communal history-making

Embedded narratives: ethnographic and heritage approaches to storytelling

In understanding historical time and "keeping" history, narrative has a central place. Narrative action may be a key to multiple, culturally specific "chronotopes" (Bakhtin 1981, 84) – landscapes of time that are not only existing but also psychologically potential and culturally inhabitable (Palmié and Stewart 2016, 218). Narrative is not only about reminiscing, bringing forth from memory; it is also an action that looks in both directions, to the past and the future, as it draws in elements of hope, expectation and difference. At the same time, narrating is an activity that touches on ethical and philosophical problems of personhood, group identity and the epistemological validity of our culturally proper sense of time (Morson 1994, 1–4). It is an activity that frames and highlights what is meaningful and important, amidst a time that can be dubbed "structural" (Braudel 1980, 104), "incremental,", "eventless" or "evolutionary" (Ingold 1986). Narrative is an eventful activity that seems to cut against the grain of most of human temporality – what earlier historiography, influenced by Hegel, saw as a blank page in history (Hegel 1974, 79).

Narrative is the stuff of heritage. Whether we acknowledge it or not, as heritage specialists we employ stories collected from the field, or we are called to create narrative sequences of our own, in descriptive texts and experience-rich presentations of our field. Large heritage institutions, however, borrow a particular sense of narrative from practical management, consumer research and corporate storytelling (cf. Schönthaler 2018, 4). This approach to narrative dilutes the complexities of local world-making and simplifies what is otherwise an ongoing process of creating meaning, fraught with incoherence, resistances, gaps, political and ethical questions. Managing difficult

DOI: 10.4324/9781003259367-5

heritage has alerted heritage professionals to the often conflicting and contested aspects of historical narratives. It remains the case, nevertheless, that the narratives offered in historical and archaeological sites and heritage institutions have a decisively "positive" character, that glosses over the multiplicity of voices, the discrepancies of recollection, and the deeply political character of storytelling.

In our case, narrative is both at the heart of making heritage, but also part of the process through which a way of being in the world has been transformed into the stuff of heritage. Most of the histories we hear in the village have to do with a way of life that has vanished. Telling histories of the past is no longer an affirmation of a way of life that has remained stable and unchanged – even if this stability was in every respect a fabrication – but a reminiscence of characteristics, mores and customs that have vanished from the life of the village. Storytelling and narrative techniques may in this respect become part of the resilience of a society, a way to maintain social bonds in the face of ongoing dissolution of community and place. Stories thus become the artifacts to be preserved, both in their formal aspect (the shape that stories take, the narrative motifs, the patterns storytellers employ), but also in their content (the place names used, the family names and nicknames employed, the remembrance of objects, places, people and customs). A word, such as the *triopatitero* weaving pattern, thus becomes an assemblage of memorial traces, linguistic indicators and bodily habitus, quite apart from their original place as functional terms in everyday usage. As heritage practitioners, we are called to provide genealogies for this rich tapestry of meaning and usage, and show the ways in which these assemblages changed form and character through larger historical transformations. It is this attention to the historical aspect of heritage artifacts that may potentially free them from being fetishized as testimonies of a stable and unchanging "tradition."

Having this critical outlook in mind, we can approach narrative for its equally positive aspects that enable practitioners in the field to open collective vistas on the past and create content that is community-controlled and richly nuanced. Heritage 'experts' should see narrative not only as a source of information about the past, but as a powerful vector for its enactment in the present. In what follows, we discuss our efforts to turn heritage work from a collection of fragmentary, incoherent, often conflicting knowledge to an inclusive collective activity.

This collective creation of knowledge about the past serves first and foremost to create new, communal stories that address what Nixon in a different context names "slow violence" (Nixon 2011), meaning here the rendering of communities, landscapes and people obsolete and the breaking down of communal ties that has resulted from decades of slowly encroaching urbanization and development. An ethnographic attention to stories and narratives also helps us understand the particular ways that the past is comprehended, and the affective aspects of temporality and historicity (Hirsch and Stewart 2005, 263) in their local specificity and in relation to dominant discourses. Ethnographic understandings of narrative strive to continuously reinsert it into the larger context of its iteration, and give it the rich cultural specificity necessary to make it legible outside any Authorized Heritage Discourse (Smith 2006 29). In order to do so, any heritage project needs to pay attention to both the ways in which a narrative is pronounced, performed, enacted and its content.

Simultaneously, we need to be aware that narratives may be occluding histories of oppression and exploitation. We propose here an alternative approach to creating such histories, by creating safe spaces where alternative narratives are evoked. By taking the notion of ethnographic installation (Castañeda 2009, 262) a step further, we are creating a sort of ethnographic dwelling, or zones of contact, into which the participation of locals creates a multiplicity of histories that are not only oral but also affective, bodily and sensuous.

A sense of time, narrative and deep time

Two youngsters, on their way to a christening, all polished and dapper, were walking to the Heraklio road, to get a ride to the ceremony and the feast to follow. On the way, they found Nikos in his car. Nikos is a remarkable storyteller and the son of a man who has acquired mythic proportions in the village for his sharp wit and self-sarcasm. Nikos had his hand in a sling, having had an accident while tending to his sheep. When the two sharp-dressed youngsters accosted him, they asked him right away what happened to his hand. Instead of giving a straight answer, Nikos began reciting: "Once, my father was going to tend to his sheep..." the two youngsters looked at each other in deep exasperation, because they were ready to go to the dance and were getting late but also because they knew that Nikos aimed to tell them the entire story first in his own, slow pace. A straight answer was not forthcoming, and the youngsters were trapped, out of politeness, and were forced to hear the story of Nikos's father out of the window of Nikos's car, parked in the middle of the street.

The aspects of this story about storytelling should alert us to the main characteristics of the importance of stories in the village. In

Gonies, as elsewhere in Crete, the verb employed to describe story-telling is not always "tell", but more often "do." One "does" a story (*kano mia istoria* – I do, or enact a story), meaning that a story is not only about its content, its plot, or its characters, but it is also about the performative ability of the teller, which needs to be employed in the present to make history happen. As the above example highlights, the temporality of the story, the pace with which the story unfolds, cannot be separated from the story itself. Storytelling is not something that happens instantaneously, but is coeval with the unfolding of the story through time, with the amount of time it takes to build up to its conclusion. The more capacious the storyteller, the slower the pace of the story as it develops. Conversely, people who have minimal ability to hold back, develop a story, keep the audience waiting for its resolution, are mocked for their lack of patience and performative prowess.

Story narration in the village is not a sequence of narrative elements – introductory scenes, reversals, suspense, etc. –, but a paratactic outlining of actions, places and people, not necessarily in the order they happened, or in the order they unfold in the memory of the teller, but also in the significance this story may have for the people present. This is further outlined by two elements of storytelling in Gonies: the first is that sentences, mini-episodes as they unfold, are connected between them by a parataxis: the word "and" connects the story and marks rhythm, much like a stomping foot would mark tempo in a group of musicians. "I went up the hill... *and* there was a goat there... *and* I recognized it to be mine... *and* I used to have a billy-goat that looked exactly like it... *and* this is why I recognized it." Verb tenses and order in time are likewise connected by "and", because *and* in this case is more than a word, it is a performative element of telling the story itself, much like a motif in epic poetry, as we are going to see below. The second element is that the punchline of the story, which is an epigrammatic phrase or a significant action, is usually used only as an anchor, which connects the story to different social situations and different telling environments.

The good storyteller is one that abides to the temporality of telling the story and not the "outside" temporality of social convention, like the haste of the two youngsters in the example above. To tell a story in its own tempo is to not be *ligopsychos* (lacking in soul – hasty). It is to stand your ground and follow the rhythm imposed by the process – whether it is milking the sheep, hammering a nail, watering the garden – means one has "soul." Soul is here taken to mean the ability to deal with what life throws at you with patience and endurance. A story frequently told of a now long deceased man, who was notorious for his slowness and love of good wine and good company, is that once his wife sent him to the neighboring village to fetch raki – the strong alcoholic distilled drink – because she was giving birth and needed it to disinfect the umbilical cord. He went to the village, found some good raki, and sat there to drink it with good company. He stayed there, some say for three days, others more, and still others exaggerate to say that by the time he got back, his son was ready to be conscripted to the army. As he was entering the house, the little flask of raki that he had around his neck caught the doorpost and broke to pieces, spilling the contents. His remark was: "this haste is going to be the end of me" (*afti I ligopsychia tha me faei*), meaning that he thought he was being too hasty for his own good coming to the village after just three days. We must have heard this story about a hundred times in the village. When it is mentioned as a common knowledge, the phrase-anchor is used as a reference, and the teller jump-cuts to it. But when it is narrated, it is important for the teller to stress the amount of time between this man's departure and his return. And this can only happen by lowering the narrative pace, interspersing other stories and descriptions, making parentheses, and long pauses. The point is to make the listener feel the time that passed between his departure and his return, rather than tell him or her of it. When the telling comes, with a sardonic remark like "his son was ready to be conscripted", it is only to mark this time spent in waiting for the story to conclude.

The written and the oral

In this respect, the histories themselves become parts of the contemporary life of the village. In the passing of time, and the gradual dissolution of the localized community, these stories are also gradually becoming objects for preservation. They become mnemonic items that have lost their original character as stories of a group of people and have gradually become indexical of a lost communal unity, however doubtful its historical existence may be. A sense of nostalgia for lost unity in place seeps into those stories. But at the same time, there is also a sense of urgency for the preservation of these tales, a transformation of these live versions into heritage items. The dialectic of oral and written, or, put in more contemporary terms, tangible and intangible forms of this heritage is crucial in this respect. We, as researchers, are entrusted by the community institutions with the preservation of such forms of memory as heritage. The expectation that is put upon us comes with a vision of monumentalizing these stories, of transforming them into an authoritative written document. It is interesting to point here the usage of the Greek word *mnimeia* (monuments) to denote written texts in early folklore studies and philology. In conversation with an elderly man from Gonies, one of the most active verse constructors in the village, he described our historical research as "writing the big book of Gonies."

When looking more closely at the way in which historical memory has been preserved and passed on, however, we quickly realize that this is not the oral society one imagines in the beginning, but that written forms of transfer are more prevalent than expected. In the summer of 2015, while driving back to Heraklio, Aris received an urgent phone call from the president of the village cultural association. He was very concerned because one of the oldest female inhabitants of the village had started dreaming that she would die soon. It was imperative that he went back to the village to interview her, because she was the only one who knew a version of the Vlachos's song that was not recorded elsewhere. Vlachos was a brigand in the middle of the nineteenth century, who is today hailed as a local hero for his resistance to the Turk oppressors. At the time that Aris received the phone call, the community was preparing the public unveiling of the statue of Vlachos that was made with municipal funds at the entrance of the village. He promptly turned his car back and went to this elderly female's house to record her reciting the epic poems that she was known for.

In conversation with her afterwards, for she lived much longer, it turned out that the poems she knew by heart were not ones she had heard anybody narrate, but written verses she had memorized from a notebook that her father had kept. Such notebooks are not rare in the village, and are a frequent occurrence in Crete in general. They usually are small school exercise books that are filled with all sorts of scribbles, from drawings to accounts, to records of things lent or borrowed, to distics created by the owner or overheard, or entire poems and reminiscences. Such exercise books are to be found in the village library or family archives, and date as far back as the nineteenth century, when Greek schools were introduced to the island. She had kept one such notebook, and, because her parents did not let her continue at school after the first three grades, she read this document continuously, until she memorized it. In the course of time, she lost this book of verses, and now her memory, already failing in her 90s, was the only repository of these written-oral poems, which were in turn recorded by us in digital form.

This coexistence of different registers and forms, from the written to the oral is not uncommon in the village. In fact, it makes for an increased communication between official forms of writing and local narratives, which is unexpected in a place where most people over their 50s or 60s only attended the first few grades of primary school. When we first began talking to the elderly in the village, we were struck at how often they could quote written sources like novels or newspaper articles by heart, interspersing their stories with such accounts. When we voiced this question, we got the answer that reading was a very popular pastime with some shepherds at least, who collected every scrap of printed paper they could lay their hands on and put it in their shoulder bag to read afterwards in the long hours of solitude while herding their sheep. To our surprise, Christos, also a shepherd in the past, was reading, when we first met him, a five-volume history of the Cuban revolution, and had just finished reading the description of the battle of Waterloo in Hugo's *les Miserables*. His verdict on Che Guevarra was damning: "he was a very bad man", but his admiration for Hugo was everlasting. He peppered his talk with quotations and sayings he had memorized from his readings, which he rendered with a tongue-in-cheek pomp to indicate that he realized the distance of the written form from everyday speech. But he was not the only one mixing the written with the oral. Anastos, in his late 80s, is a writer of distics, which he publishes in book form and also sends to newspaper or radio station competitions. Dimitris, a recently deceased miller from the village, kept an "archive", as people recall it, which consists of a variety of diaries, journals, and specially consigned notebooks, such as the one he kept for the biggest lies ever told in the village. The understanding of the officiating nature of archive-keeping in written form is amply illustrated in a story told in the village of one person who told a tall story, and then, realizing that Dimitris was present, turned to him and urged him: "do not write it down!" He laughingly decried, "you shouldn't have told it then!"

Finally, the relationship between written and oral becomes reciprocal in unexpected ways. Stylianos Alexiou, the excavator of Philioremos we encountered in the first chapter, was also the editor of one of the best known, and perhaps the best, epic poems of renaissance Crete, *Erotokritos* by Vicenzo Cornaro. We do not know whether Alexiou was aware that Gonies was the ownership of distant strands of the Cornaro family in the fifteenth century, but it is documented that he edited the poem by collecting words from the Cretan dialect of his time. It is possible therefore that the usage of the people of the village was something that Alexiou took back with him along with the material found on Philioremos.

Official commemoration

The intermingling of written and oral sources, with the production of memory in the confines of national unification is nowhere more evident that in the instance of the official commemoration of the village-born nineteenth century brigand Michalis Vlachos. Vlachos is an almost mythical personality, born in the early nineteenth century with the surname Kalisperis or Kalisperakis. Still very young, he displayed a marked insubordination and headed a gang comprising both Christian and Muslim Cretans, who attacked mostly rich Muslim landlords to steal their money, goods and animals. The official state dealt with Vlachos as a common criminal, and sentenced him to death on the 16th of February 1857 for the murder of a Muslim landlord and the theft of his property. The Christians of the island, however, mostly through long epic songs, inaugurated this personality into the "last of the Cretan Chainis (brigands)" and presented his activity as glorious feats in the national struggle for liberation from the Ottoman Turks. Vlachos participated in the failed 1841 insurrection against the regime, and remained in hiding for a good decade before he was arrested and executed (Stavrinidis 1980, 17–9).

In the early 1980s, the Cultural Association of the village urged the director of the Turkish archive in Vikelea Municipal library of Iraklio, Nikos Stavrinidis, to republish a series of articles he had written on Vlachos in booklet form. The booklet came out in 1980, funded by the association, and has been in wide circulation ever since. Stavrinidis's archival research put the definitive seal of reality on the oral narratives that had been preserved intact in the village and elsewhere for more than a century. The discovery of semi-mythical characters like Vlachos in the archive makes for a conglomerate of oral tradition and archival history that is deeply ambiguous. On the one hand, the officiating practice of the historian renders the experiential and deeply affective practice of the local poet authoritative. This seal of approval, however, reveals the deep power inequalities that exist and are reproduced within the historical practices of the nation state. While both approaches share an affective engagement with unilinear national narratives, that present every attack against Muslims as part of the irredentist struggle against the Turks and conceal centuries of peaceful coexistence, at the same time, the historian's approach is closer to "acceptable" historical narratives in the confines of the national state. The historian has the power to put the local history of the place into the national narrative.

Seen from the vantage point of the village, any mention in historical accounts strengthens the position of the village in national narratives of liberation and increases its "importance." This understanding aims to establish the participation of villagers in key events in the Cretan struggle for enosis (union) with Greece in the nineteenth century, as well as the resistance movement against Axis invasion during the World War II. Thus, localities are not just geographical territories or value-free neutral landscapes, instead they are contested communities in historically produced social contexts discerned by agency and sociality. The local here is understood as an active agent capable of engaging with "the social activities of production, representation, and reproduction" of (national) meanings and social contexts (Appadurai 1995; Herzfeld 2003). Nevertheless, this strategic consideration should not blind us to the affective content that locality brings to officially sanctioned forms of commemoration.

In 2016, the municipality of Malevizi funded a statue to Vlachos placed at the entrance of a village. The bronze work, created by a Herakliot sculptor commissioned by public competition, was hailed as a long-due recognition of the participation of the village to the national struggles for liberation from the Turks, as a necessary inscription of local historical personalities to the official national narrative. At the same time, however, the statue itself became an effigy that introduced its uncanny bodily presence to the village. Mrs. Eleftheria, driving up from the sheep den in her husband's car, always saluted the statue with a "to your health Captain!" (*Geia sou kapetanie*). Others commented on the rather diminutive size of the statue, especially in contrast with the larger than human size statues of similar personalities in adjacent villages. A discussion ensued regarding the bodily size of inhabitants of the area in the past, which brought to mind the vest of a local warlord kept in public display at the only functional cafe in Kamariotis, an abandoned village nearby. This vest would easily fit a young adolescent, making it a testimony to the diminutive size of even the most ferocious personalities of past history. This discussion, waged on the borderline of aloofness toward public embarrassment from potential detractors, also humanizes official versions of heritage. The personal link between material expressions of nationalist pride acquire their significant effectiveness from this potent affective relationship. This should alert us to the weight that these material artifacts acquire for a community and their ability to solidify otherwise fluid interpretations of the past with their presence. It is an important realization for heritage experts who strive toward a more inclusive version of local heritage, memory and history.

The dialectics of forgetfulness

Aris is sitting down on the bend of a rock with an elderly shepherd, snacking on olives and cheese from a nylon bag. They have followed the length of the path he had taken with his sheep, after his insistence. He wanted to show him his turf, but also we suspect he was looking for the opportunity to visit familiar places of his youth for one last time. He is ecstatic, but very tired. Sitting down and eating picks him up a bit, and he starts telling some stories. Most of his stories have violent endings, with people being maimed or killed in one way or another. Above them, hang the sharp edges of a cliff, peppered with green patches of bush. He begins a story of a murder that happened exactly in that spot. He recounts it with a surprising matter-of-factness, given that he was a firsthand witness, and almost got killed in the fray. Aris remains stunned for a while, unsure what question to ask next. The very description has frozen him, not with the violent content, but with the coolness of the narrator, who told the story with the detachment of someone describing a visit to the greengrocer's. He is slowly pulling himself together, when some other shepherds arrive, guiding their flock to higher ground. It is summer, and the animals are moved from lower, warmer pastures to the now lush green mountains to graze. They stop and talk for a while, and Aris forgets the whole story. He never mentions it on the way back, either. But the next day, he decides to clarify some details. Over coffee, he asks him again, how about that guy who was murdered in that place over there? The answer is a blank stare, a blunt "what do you mean?" and to his insistence, a series of evasions "Who? I do not know what you are talking about." In his naivety, Aris was left baffled by the incomprehension that ensued, and went back to his notes of the day to make sure he had really heard the story. It was all there, in some detail. At the beginning, he believed that his interlocutor's memory was failing him, but his persistence at other instances gradually warned him to a different explanation: he was simply refusing to repeat his story. Perhaps he got carried away by his enthusiasm and the shared moment and told a story he was not supposed to tell. Later on, this story vanished, just like many other stories in the course of our ethnographic research in the village.

We have withheld the name of our interlocutor and any details of the story he had told. While his refusal to acknowledge the telling of this story is there, it is this refusal, and not the story in itself that is important in the course of research about the past. Anthropologists as of late have turned their attention to ethnographic refusal as an ethical position from which collaborative research can be constructed (see e.g. McGranahan 2016; Simpson 2007, 2014). Simply put, such refusal may amount to collectively, either explicitly or through a tacit agreement, decide which stories can be told and which cannot. Structuring research on the basis of heritage, where presence is much more central than absence, where stories, things and persons need to be brought forward and not held in the shadow, refusals such as these constitute blank spots for practitioners. Recent work on difficult heritage, however, has alerted practitioners to the gaps and silences and refusals as constitutive elements of the way difficult memories are construed and worked through in the present, therefore as important aspects of how a group of people remembers, that need to be considered in order to understand the shape of social memory in the present (see Arnold-de-Simine 2013).

We are recounting this example to show how a culture that promotes secrecy and strictly regulates the flow of stories and information influences collective memory at large. What is noticeable about Gonies is the relatively shallow genealogical memory, even of the most elderly inhabitants. On the contrary, their knowledge of genealogical ties is richly detailed, even for other families than their own. While knowledge of the present is therefore a predominant social factor in the village, there seems to be some impediment in its transmission across generations. As they themselves tell it, "the older generations did not talk much about it at all." One elderly interlocutor complained about his father not telling him any "stories" at all. "He never talked to me about anything", he said, "not even our own heroic ancestors." His great grandfather had fought in at least one Cretan insurrection, but very few things are known of him. This lack of information is generally hailed in the coffee shops of the village as a deep modesty that characterizes the place. Goniotes, it is said, have made heroic deeds, but they have refused to promote them publicly, contrary to what people from nearby villages have done, and therefore they were left out of official inscriptions of history. Much deeper than that, however, there is this culture of silence which constructs a noticeable collective forgetting (Connerton 1989, 35; Forty and Küchler 1999). Our interlocutor's father, who refused to tell him stories, was himself a very well-respected shepherd in the area, which meant he was one of the few persons that would be called to resolve feuds between shepherds, often ensuing from animal theft. His silence was not simply a refusal to say things about other people, it was an integral part of his status in the society he lived in. He was not a man to tell stories, and precisely that made him averse to recounting in general.

The apparently shallow memory of Goniotes is unsurprisingly linked to a series of stories of displacement and feud. A very common narrative links these displacements with acts of insubordination against the "Turks", meaning the Ottoman authorities or Muslim notables. The most common story is that an ancestor who killed a local Muslim notable was forced to flee to the mountains to avoid capture, finally ending up in Gonies. But what is remarkable is that stories of displacement which are probably true, since Goniote shepherds frequently had quite a spot of trouble with the law well into the twentieth century (Papadakis 2010), were turned into stories of origin. In the summer of 2014, Aris managed to locate a reference in the Venetian archive to the surname of a local family of the village. It placed ancestors of the family in the area at least all the way back to 1618. We reached one of the younger members of the family, and president of the cultural association of the village, to announce this discovery. His surprise was evident. Not only did they not have a memory of their presence in the village, but their family story had it that they were quite new to it, having moved very recently into Gonies from Messara, in a move led by a *kapetanios* (insurgent chief) called Pouli Giorgis in the nineteenth century.

How does that shallowness of memory influence the way people think about locality and time? What surprised us when we first came to Gonies was that very few, if any, Goniotes would claim an ancestry from Minoan stock. Trained as we were to expect such claims to continuity from other parts of Greece, we discovered few traces of it here. Perhaps the secondary position attributed to Minoan antiquity in the Greek national hierarchy of value plays a role in this. Simply put, the emphasis of the national narrative on cultural (and racial) continuity, claims its importance, and its imagery, from classical antiquity. Other civilizations, such as the Minoan, are considered "pre-hellenic", taking the lineage of modern Greeks, and therefore their claim over their national land, even further back in time. However, this pre-hellenic aspect is never as important in its imagery or narrative in the way that the Authorized Heritage Discourse is managed centrally. In Crete at large, this pre-hellenic claim comes to underwrite a sense of local pride, in establishing Crete as the birthland of Greek civilization (cf. Hamilakis and Momigliano 2006).

Looking more closely into the way locals connect to the land and place, we realized that although there are stories of settlement that reach deep in time, the sense of continuity, carried by genealogical memory, is quite shallow. What is in place is a feeling of habitation of the place by people in the *longue duree*. This is evident by the place names of the area, most of which draw from ancient words and signify places of Minoan settlement, like names ending in –sos, e.g. Kanasos, that display evidence of Minoan remains (Kyriakidis 2012). There is therefore a sense of presence in the area for millennia, but not a strong sense of any sort of ancestry. We would say that the link to the deep temporality of this place comes not from – the usual in Greece – sense of "blood" continuity, i.e. racially inflected biological time, but the temporality of the landscape itself. The human landscape is recognized as very old and carries with it the sense of human presence in the area, which Goniotes understand and incorporate in their relationship to the land.

More recent events feature most prominently in the reminiscences of the current inhabitants of the village. Traumatic stories from the German occupation of the island are central in life histories of elderly individuals. Gradually, those stories about the World War II are turned into heroic feats by younger generations who retell them. The participation of Goniotes in both the struggle of liberation of Crete in the nineteenth century and the resistance movement against the Axis powers becomes an important anchor point for the reworking of live memories and their inscription into national unilinear narratives.

Bringing historical narratives to the fore

The ubiquity of storytelling as a means to remember but also reshape the past and make it relevant to the present was not lost to us during our fieldwork. The necessity to make a new narrative about the village that comes to terms with the, sometimes traumatic, effects of the recent past was evident and instrumental in shaping the future of the village. The profusion of stories and the emphasis on the telling and retelling the history of the recent past gradually turned our focus toward the more recent heritage of the village, as has been discussed elsewhere in this book. But at the same time, it changed the way we approached ethnographic fieldwork, by turning our attention more toward the ways in which this past is framed and reframed through life stories.

As an inherent part of our ethnographic work in the village, we did a series of formal or informal interviews throughout the years. While our focus was initially the relationships of locals to the remains of the ancient past, interviews were open-ended from the beginning. We wanted to allow our interlocutors to tell us what was more important to them, to structure the discussion around the most prominent themes in their lives. As our intimacy and trust with locals grew stronger, the interviews changed their character from focused questions about the material aspects of heritage and the ancient past toward longer life narratives, that focused on important events in the recent history of the village: the German occupation, the pressures of immigration, the effort to rejuvenate the village. As this process progressed, we were faced with the more daunting task of recording and safeguarding the memories of villagers that were still alive and creating a common pool of knowledge that was shared with all interested parties. This safekeeping acquired sometimes a very urgent character, as valuable knowledge was in danger of getting lost forever.

At the same time, processes of historical commemoration in the village brought into focus our archival research and questioned our ability to make historical knowledge of a more technical, but also more fragmented form freely available in the village. The main conundrum faced when conducting a public history strategy for the village is that we do not want to create with our actions an essentialist reading of history, one that aids villagers to reinsert themselves into a national(ist) narrative or that reinforces such readings. Simultaneously, it is a permanent question of our research how to undermine the 'expert'-audience power relationships by engaging locals in this research. To begin with the latter, it is not easy at all, given the difficulty of access to historical archives in Crete and Greece at large. Although a program of research involving locals would be a good aim for a research project such as ours, this is very difficult given that the archives in Heraklio are not catalogued, and historical research necessarily turns into a slow process of collecting tidbits of information, a systematic scanning of a massive volume of documents for relevant names and placenames that may in the end constitute a coherent historical narrative, or they may not.

On the other hand, the collusion of oral memories and historical evidence in the archive produces a new field for collaboration in the creation of historical knowledge, as well as an opportunity to control the writing of local history. A lost reference to an Ottoman religious court decision found in the card index of the late director of the Turkish Archive in the Vikelea Municipal library in Heraklio, for example, turns into a historical item that evokes memories, discussions and disputes and begins a process of historical thinking that ultimately involves the whole village. Nikos Stavrinidis, the scholar already mentioned above has produced a number of volumes of translations of the Ottoman archive in Heraklio (known as the Turkish Archive), that he directed for decades. In the loose papers of his office there is an index card file, that bears a single reference to Gonies, and in particular to a dispute on the water of Sklavokampos between Gonies and a neighboring village, Korfes, quite possibly in 1875. As much as we, and other colleagues, have looked in the archive, we were unable to locate the reference to the religious court decision on the index card. The painstaking work of revisiting the sources is then returned to the locals themselves: we went there, copy of the card in hand, and asked which possible event it may refer to. Gradually, through discussions, an old story resurfaced, whereby the great-grandfather of a living Goniote had been involved in an exchange of insults with a person from the neighboring village, which resulted in the youngster from Gonies stabbing the Korfiote to death. Locals recited the dialogue that led up to the stabbing, quite possibly enriched and elaborated through the years, and asserted that it was the audacity of this youngster that sealed the control of the water once and for all in favor of the village. Several shepherds have walked up with us to the remote water source of Sykia, placing the archive mention as a real landscape feature.

Thus, oral history and the ensuing discussions have turned archival work into a collaborative work of knowledge production, and even corrected the nomenclature of historical archives: Stavrinidis noted the water as that of Sklavokampos. The locals insist that the correct name is the water of the Sykia source. We are divided between proper historical referencing and the demands of locals for the reinstitution of the correct names in the sources. In July 2018, we presented at the end of the summer school the result of a six-year historical research on the village in the form of a timeline, written in plain language. The relevant card mentioning this source carried the name of Sklavokampos, as it was written on the index card. This caused vocal protests from quite some locals, who pointed out that this is "a serious historical mistake" that needs to be corrected. It was difficult to explain to them that this is how the source mentions it, and we cannot intervene to change it, but that their accounts may serve to restate this reference in a historical way.

Narratives about the past evoked through embodied methods: art and craft as powerful evocative techniques

The presentation and analysis offered above leads us to a double conclusion: first, the way that the past is remembered, as well as the content of this remembrance are not always *there*, in the sense that they can be observed and recorded by a researcher. Most often, they are part of a tacit knowledge that contains many layers, some of them hidden, consciously or unconsciously. Thus, history and historicity, as the sense of the passage of time and of the importance of past events, has to be evoked to be studied. Ethnographic methods create the spaces in which such an evocation of the past can happen in a dialogic and collaborative way, often leading to unexpected results as will be evident in the example that follows. The second conclusion is that such evocations of historical events and processes are necessarily performative. That is, they require the presence of bodies in space, they are transformed by this presence, and they are channeled through a theatricality that places as heavy an emphasis on aspects of the telling (theatricality, parataxis, suspense, punchlines, development in time) as on the content of the stories themselves. Incidents such as these mentioned above directed us to devise more inclusive way of dealing with heritage and history. Looking at the performative potential of public events and how these events may serve as grounds for the collaborative creation of historical knowledge, we have created the conditions for similar performative events. In what follows, we are going to present in some length and analyze our engagement with public art and the engagement of locals through crafts, in a setting that is based on the idea of "ethnographic installation" (Castañeda 2009) but takes it a step further through the concerns and experience of contemporary art and curating.

Castañeda notes that ethnographic installations are actions that on a first look resemble public outreach activities, in that these events aim to give back to the subjects of ethnographic fieldwork the knowledge gleaned from them – from the researchers themselves or from other persons and institutions in the past. The important difference is that an ethnographic installation involves the staging of ethnographic research as part of the presentation. In such setups, the researchers, artists or ethnographers, do not try to impose a specific meaning or narrative on the knowledge of the past. Instead, they choose to make this past present in an open-ended way – a way that facilitates its reappropriation by community members that have a stake in this past (Castañeda 2009, 266). To this well-intended means of creating collaborative occasions of knowledge creation, we add the element of the researcher as curator.

In the presentation of ethnographic and historical work in Gonies, the research team continuously attempted to engage members of the community in research and presentation. The final product aimed for was not a unique narrative, but a "curating" of many different stories, objects and places, in order to incorporate a plurality of voices. Even so, the final product of this research, be it a walking tour, a heritage path, a temporary exhibition, displayed an amount of coherence in narrative, even if this was created by visitors themselves. We experiment by putting in place what has been called "ethnographic installations" that create spaces where "things happen, stories unfold, people meet and discuss, works are produced, possibilities are created" (Konstantinou and Anagnostopoulos 2019). This is a process that itself becomes the focus of the work and diverts our attention from the finished product (a book, an exhibition, an artwork) to what happens in the here and now, in the field. "The process is not, or not only, the evocation of a historical experience, a past already there; but also a meeting ground between the embodied, sensuous knowledge of the past and our formal, social-scientific and historical methods of approaching it." (Konstantinou and Anagnostopoulos 2019)

In July 2016, we put in practice an experimental fieldwork practice by inviting locals to participate in an open artist studio. The visual artist Alexia Karavela, curated by the curator and art historian Katerina Konstantinou, set up a weaving workshop in one of the disused halls of the primary school of the village (Figure 4.1). We intended to set up a situation that would evoke embodied memories and create a safe space for the communal creation of knowledge. The open studio was based on the work that Katerina had already done with us as a participant in the 2015 summer school. Beginning with a notion of weaved textiles as tangible heritage, embedded within a static notion of traditional produce common in Crete and Greece, Katerina slowly began unearthing hidden histories and embodied transcripts of exploitation and resistance to the demands of mass production. Local women were invited to come and visit the open studio and collaborate with Alexia in creating a communally weaved cloth. But this involved a series of moment of collaboration, from finding and transporting the looms (which were donated by people in the village) to setting them up, stringing them, working them and removing the final product. This resulted in a month-long "zone of engagement" (Onciul 2015), an open space for the exchange of knowledge, skill and critical dialogue on what constitutes tradition, heritage and the tacit histories of "traditional" production in the region.

Woven textiles were commonly produced by women in every household, as part of the preparation of dowries, but equally importantly to cater for the needs of the household in cloth, linen and bed covers. Until at least the late decades of the twentieth century, every household owned a loom, which was worked by the women of the house, producing cloth and embroidered artifacts. Weaved textiles nowadays are stored in naphthalene-protected wooden caskets and only taken out for interested visitors – some are of such great quality and

Figure 4.1 The artistic workshop setup in a classroom of the old village school. Photo: Katerina Konstantinou.

craftmanship that are framed and hung on house walls. All looms have been dismantled and either thrown away or stored. Nobody in the village operates a loom nowadays. Thus, weaving has progressed from being a part of the everyday chores of a household to being an iconic item in traditional heritage.

The dominant heritage discourses on weaving in rural Crete have created the "Cretan loom" as a unique object that testifies to the cultural continuity of Cretans throughout history and also evidences the exceptionality of the island in comparison to other areas in Greece. Such looms are as a norm compared with similar looms used in antiquity, mostly based on archaeological findings of loom-weights. A common assertion of such approaches is that the practice of weaving and the development of the particular form of loom has continued uninterrupted from Minoan times to the twentieth century. It is seen as a survival from ancient forms of looms, although there are no significant differences from looms that have been in use in other parts of Europe for centuries. At least since the late decades of the nineteenth century, the rural woman has been explicitly tied to picturesque renditions in the visual arts and literature with the seated loom and has been rendered as iconic of traditional village life, in a process that inextricably ties female identities with nationalist projects of national unification (cf. Anagnostopoulos 2014).

The looms themselves, their construction and function, have been rendered in detail in folklore studies of rural populations all over Greece. The same is true for weaving motifs and patterns, such as the *triopatitero*, which is also known locally. Such studies have usually depicted local populations as "domestic exotics" within the sovereign national state (Herzfeld 1987: 10). Folklore studies have developed a very strong critical strand in the recent years, yet the study of weaving (see for example a recent publication Michelogiannaki-Karavelaki 2015) as well as other aspects of village technical production are still rendered as a stable, unchanging folklore object and studied in an unreflexively. This is certainly one of the dangers that heritagization may pose for the creation of communal knowledge about the past. Transforming the material and immaterial aspects of a complex process of production and exploitation with incredibly rich relationships developing between human and non-human subjects into a heritage object may fetichize this process and restore it in an idealized past. Such renderings on the one hand occlude the internal colonization of peoples from the national intelligentsia inherent in older folklore studies; on the other, they turn narratives of oppression and exploitation into esthetically rich, coherent and seemingly benign forms of "traditional craft."

Weaving in wooden looms has been portrayed in folkloric renditions with rosy colors, as a female pastime and creative outlet that encapsulated the notion of "a people." Much emphasis is paid on the ability of women weavers to tap a rich source of traditional motifs and create regional variations that testified both to the vitality of local places and the creativity of local populations within national traditions. Nowadays, such discourses are worked back into a resurgence of local artisanal craft as new forms of sustainable tourism develop. However, both the narratives evoked during the open studio, and the visceral reactions and bodily stances of women who came to participate, alerted us to an entirely different, and largely hidden story of an otherwise rosy traditional female occupation. It is true that most women were eager to demonstrate their technical skill and artistry and quickly fell into their well-known patterns of competitive weaving and the bragging associated with it. At the same time, most of them declared from the beginning that they hated working on the loom. Some went as far to say that they wanted to burn their old looms and forget that they ever weaved at all. It transpired that weaving was a forced task, including truly backbreaking work that consumed a very large part of their adolescent and adult life. Weaving was imposed on women not only by dire need, but also by the pressure to create their own dowry goods and secure a successful marriage, perhaps a profitable one for the family and certainly one that proved its social standing. Weaving was therefore an arduous task that was added to the many daily female tasks of keeping up the household. In the post-war era, this task was commercialized by the tourist industry. Women from nearby villages acted as intermediaries of big companies that employed artisanal work paid by the piece. We were able to corroborate this story from loose receipts and letters discovered in abandoned houses of the village. It turned out that these networks of artisanal production not only drew on local craft production, but also transformed its output, controlled its quality and intensified production. This development certainly transformed women unexpectedly into money makers for the household, who contributed their meagre earnings to those of agricultural and livestock production. However, this did not mean a significant change for their social status, as it intensified their manual work, and imposed an almost industrial discipline to their production, with deadlines, quota and quality benchmarks imposed by traders and women acting as intermediaries.

The richness and complexity of those narratives were a surprise to us as researchers, simply because they are never available to anyone who approaches weaving for its folkloristic or heritage value. At the same time, those were not narratives that could be gleamed by direct ethnographic interviewing, since those occasions were detached from the actual process of weaving. It almost seemed that the very practice of weaving as a bodily activity, recreated during the open studio, brought to the surface embodied memories that were later transformed into words. This happened only gradually, and the looms acted as objects that jogged the memories of these women to produce layers upon layers of rich historical discourses that unsettled the established image of traditional weaving and crafts.

The importance of embodied memories was not restricted to women themselves. We were aiming to create safe spaces for women of the village to congregate, share and discuss. The idea of such spaces was a cut in the social mores of the village, where women can gather in houses, on appropriate social occasions and in church or the elderly day care center, but not in any other social spaces. This workshop simply provided an adequate reason for them to exist together in public, and they made the most of it. However, contrary to our expectations, there were also many men who paid short visits to the open studio and also tried their hand at the loom, although the whole process is exclusively associated with women and female labor. The reason all these men gave for their presence there was the strong childhood memories associated with the weaving process and their mothers. Most mentioned the characteristic repetitive crack of the loom as one of their strongest early memories, and many recalled with welling tears instances where their mothers entrusted them with threading the clews for the loom.

While for men bodily memories were the avenue to a distant idealized past, however, for most women it was a trigger for the evocation

Figure 4.2 Setting up one of the looms used in the workshop. Photo: Katerina Konstantinou.

of memories and narratives that complicated the historical picture of traditional crafts in the region. All the participants concluded that the advent of tourism on the island of Crete was a turning point in turning weaving and traditional crafts in general into a low-intensity industry for mass markets. Mass production was quickly organized through networks of acquaintances; women from nearby Anogia or in Heraklio would buy off bulk artifacts from women in the village for a token price, and then sell them wholesale to traders in Athens. This process was very much connected with a standardization process of local artisanal production began by the Greek state at around the end of the 1950s – the Office for Regional Development of the then Ministry of Coordination, for example, performed a state-wide inventory of crafts and craft-makers, to be used by the National Organization of Greek Crafts.

This development quickly transformed production from use-oriented cloth to standardized, commissioned items. It changed first and foremost the quality of material produced and its use-value; "traditional" cloths were primarily used in everyday homemaking, but their touristic materialization chiefly promoted them as decorative. Accordingly, the motifs weaved on commercial cloths changed. The most significant change was the introduction of motifs representing iconic Minoan archaeological discoveries, such as the "prince of lilies" fresco at Knossos. This fresco was re-created from parts of frescoes discovered in Knossos around 1905, and represents a young "prince" with distinctive headgear walking among lilies (Gere 2009, 121). An iconic figure of the Minoan representational universe, it was first described by Sir Arthur Evans as a "Priest King" in the first volume of *The Palace of Minos*, and later came to symbolize the whole publationa dn excavation project, adoring the cover of successive tomes of the book series (Gere 2009, 119–20). To the minds of local weavers who first got to work on this pattern through for market purposes, it came to represent king Minos himself, who purportedly crossed the village during his pilgrimage to mount Ida. We see there that circuitous route through which archaeological representations can be (re)introduced into the life of a local place and acquire the status of an "invented tradition" that may, ironically, be used to demonstrate deep antiquity for such populations.

The performative iterations of body movements in this zone of engagement brought to the fore personal stories that together spelled the picture of a profound social transformation and the frequently traumatic reactions to it. Creating this performative space provided an eventful place that evoked and supported the expression of critical histories of the past, and reframed the collective memory of the community. Wooden looms are preserved in the village as a nostalgic indicator of a life past that may be perceived as onerous, backward and difficult, but also is loaded with a nostalgic yearning for community and a sense of future prospects. The final product of this process is an idealized image of the past as a rich repository of more authentic, traditional ways of life. This image is supported materially by the presence of such objects as looms. As it became evident in the first few days of the project, there are many dismantled looms in the village, some stored mainly for their value as heritage, but basically defunct without the deep embodied knowledge of their past users. As objects on their way to become heritage artifacts, looms are also attractors of bodily techniques that cannot be transferred to later generations, who have had no experience of the workings of such looms, except in a performative mode. The first few days of the studio were spent in a hapless effort to set up the first loom, mainly based on visual memory and pictures of similar looms. One day, Mrs. Erasmia walked in and confronted the jumble of parts, rods and strings that Katerina and Alexia had set up with the help of some younger local men. She immediately exclaimed "but this is all wrong!" After Katerina asked her how to set this up properly, she did not answer anything, but grabbed a piece of string and, smiling while looking at them in the eyes, quickly took the measurements of the diagonals of the loom (Figure 4.2). She then ordered, push this side of the frame hither! And suddenly the loom was in perfect alignment, eliciting her triumphant smile.

The open studio had sufficient time, ample space and demanded a lot of care to keep it open, accessible and sustain the interest and engagement of the women and men who came to visit on a daily basis. Perhaps the most arduous task was to sustain the openness of the place, which meant that the capabilities and demands of the researchers and artists who voluntarily staffed it had to be attuned to the rhythms and capabilities of the community. Different people made different use of the space; elderly women had to make time between household chores and were able to mobilize their networks of friends to transform the disused school into a meeting place. Opening the place was not sufficient to draw them in, a constant communication by telephone had to be sustained as well. It transpired that the preparations to come to the studio, the long series of mutual phone calls and arrangements were as important as their presence there. As we discuss in the following chapter, we initially understood this as a form of resistance and refusal. Yet, through this process, we came to reframe our view and see how the mobilization itself, taken up in this case by the women of the village, was an central part of engagement, as the work necessary to build social bonds, muster the energies and capacities of the group and negotiate the form and direction of the process. Urged by our academic culture and in sync with the outlook of artistic production that focuses on the finished product, the "work", we struggled to keep our attention to the flux and flurry of arrangements, negotiations, communications, cancellations and mediations that, it seems to us now, constitute the very work of engaging a community.

At the conclusion of the studio, we puzzled over finding a way to communicate in a shared way its basic contours and highlight this important element of collaboration. In discussion with a group of local youngsters, we decided to turn the final presentation into a song. At that time, the village was buzzing with the publication by the Smithsonian archive of a recording made in the village by the Swiss ethnomusicologist Samuel Baud-Bovy in 1954 (Baud-Bovy 2006). One of the songs that caught the attention of younger musicians was a ballad performed with a wooden flute by a legendary personality of the village, one Nathenogiannis. The ballad was a love song describing the return of a migrant to his home and the ensuing dialogue with his wife, and was then being reworked into the repertoire of the local players as a piece particular to the village. In informal meetings in the studio, we reworked the lyrics of the song to describe the setting up of the studio, paying great attention to the role of women in animating it and supporting its work. The song was sung at the village meeting at the end of the project, instead of a textual or visual presentation and was quickly adopted by the younger generation and sung as part of their nightly gatherings with music.[1]

In sum, the employment of art projects and multimodal methods of research created very active occasions where knowledge was created and shared in a communal way. Two aspects of this process need to be recapped here: one is that narrative, both as a mode of understanding time and as the stuff of intangible heritage, is not something that is "there" and just needs to be picked with the right recording tools. Narrative is performative, contextual and multilayered. Instead, therefore, of the usual methods of recording it, practitioners in the field may think about creating ethnographic situations where such narratives are evoked, acted out and collectively discussed in critical ways. This results in rich accounts of past life and heritage, but also creates new social bonds, or strengthens existing ones, in the here and now. The second aspect that we need to highlight is the way in which such spaces and events need to be attuned to the local context and not imposed from outside. A long process of ethnographic research and understanding is necessary in organizing such meetings and creating content that is accessible, recognizable and manageable by the communities involved.

Note

1. Both versions of the song can be found at https://www.youtube.com/watch?v=mTV0IXPhWCk and https://www.youtube.com/watch?v=_S3PrZik4fM.

References

Anagnostopoulos, Aris. 2014. Writing the Cretan Woman. Gender and Society in Two Ethographies of Fin-de-siècle Crete. *Journal of Modern Greek Studies* 32 (1): 81–110.

Appadurai, Arjun. 1995. "The Production of Locality." In: Richard Fardon (ed.), *Counterworks: Managing the Diversity of Knowledge*. London: Routledge, 204–25.

Arnold-de-Simine, Silke. 2013. *Mediating Memory in the Museum: Trauma, Empathy, Nostalgia*. Basingstoke: Palgrave Macmillan.

Bakhtin, Mikhail. 1981. *The Dialogic Imagination: Four Essays*. Austin and London: University of Texas Press.

Baud-Bovy, Samuel. 2006. *Mousiki katagrafi stin Kriti 1953-54*. Edited by Lambros Liavas. Athens: Centre for Asia Minor Studies - Musical Folklore Archives Melpo Merlie.

Braudel, Fernand. 1980. *On History*. Translated by Sarah Matthews. Chicago: University of Chicago Press.

Castañeda, Quetzil. 2009. "The 'Past' as Transcultural Space: Using Ethnographic Installation in the Study of Archaeology." *Public Archaeology* 8 (2-3): 262–82.

Connerton, P. 1989 [2003]. *How Societies Remember*. Cambridge: Cambridge University Press.

Forty, Adrian and Küchler, Susanne (eds.). 1999. *The Art of Forgetting*. Oxford: Berg.

Gere, Cathy. 2009. *Knossos and the Prophets of Modernism*. Chicago, IL: University of Chicago Press.

Hamilakis, Yannis and Nicoletta Momigliano (eds.). 2006. *Archaeology and European Modernity: Producing and Consuming the Minoans*. *Creta Antica 7*. Padova: Bottega d' Erasmo.

Hegel, Georg. 1974. *Lectures on the Philosophy of World History*. Cambridge, MA: Cambridge University Press.

Herzfeld, Michael. 2003. "Localism and the Logic of Nationalistic Folklore: Cretan Reflections." *Comparative Studies in Society and History* 45: 281–310.

Herzfeld, Michael. 1987. *Anthropology Through the Looking-Glass: Critical Ethnography in the Margins of Europe*. Cambridge: Cambridge University Press.

Hirsch, Eric and Charles Stewart. 2005. Introduction: Ethnographies of Historicity. *History and Anthropology* 16 (3): 261–74.

Ingold, Tim. 1986. *Evolution and Social Life*. Cambridge, MA: Cambridge University Press.

Konstantinou, Katerina and Aris Anagnostopoulos. 2019. "Interweaving contemporary art and 'traditional' crafts in ethnographic research". *Art/Research International: A Transdisciplinary Journal* 4 (1): 58–82.

Kyriakidis, Evangelos. 2012. "Borders and Territories: The Borders of Classical Tylissos." *Cambridge Classics Journal [Online]* 58: 115–144.

McGranahan, Carol. 2016. "Theorizing Refusal: An Introduction." *Cultural Anthropology* 31 (3): 319–25.

Michelogiannaki-Karavelaki, Atalanti. 2015. *Yfainontas stin Kriti*. [Weaving in Crete.] Heraklion: Itanos.

Morson, Gary Saul. 1994. *Narrative and Freedom. The Shadows of Time*. New Haven, CT: Yale University Press.

Nixon, Rob. 2011. *Slow Violence and the Environmentalism of the Poor*. Cambridge, MA: Harvard University Press.

Onciul, Bryony. 2015. *Museums, Heritage and Indigenous Voice: Decolonizing Engagement*. New York, NY: Routledge.

Palmié, Stephan and Charles Stewart. 2016. "Introduction: For an Anthropology of History." *HAU: Journal of Ethnographic Theory* 6 (1): 207–36.

Papadakis, Manolis. 2001. *Gonies. Ena taksidi sto chrono kai sto choro*. Thessaloniki: Ekdoseis Aplatanos.

Schönthaler, Philip. 2018. *Portrait of the Manager as a Young Author: On Storytelling, Business, and Literature.* Cambridge, MA: The MIT Press.

Simpson, Audra. 2007. "Ethnographic Refusal: Indigeneity, 'Voice' and Colonial Citizenship." *Junctures: The Journal for Thematic Dialogue* 9: 67–80. http://junctures.org/index.php/junctures/issue/view/11/showToc.

Simpson, Audra. 2014. *Mohawk Interruptus: Political Life across the Borders of Settler States.* Durham, NC: Duke University Press.

Smith, Laurajane. 2006. *Uses of Heritage.* London: Routledge.

Stavrinidis, Nikolaos. 1980. *Michalis Vlachos. O Teleftaios Chainis kai to Tragiko Telos tou.* Iraklio: n.p.

5 Looking reflexively at community engagement

The examples of collaborative research and community engagement presented in this book are shared in the expectation that they will add to the discussion on the hows and whys of working with local communities in the fields of archaeology and heritage. We came to the field with some preconceived notions, experiences and expectations, and, as with any open process, we left with more questions and only a few certainties. We believe that part of the scholarly work involved in reflecting and conceptualizing field experience is to pose these questions adequately so that they can be answered in particular settings and contexts. So what we would like to do here is to pose some of the persistent questions that arise from our work. The first set of questions has to do with the content and ethics of our own motivations. What is expected by our definition of engagement? What do we consider a successful engagement? What is our explicit or implicit goal? Why do engagement to begin with? What do locals think about it, and how would they like to be engaged, if at all?

There is also the question who gets engaged in community engagement and how. Do we engage through local institutions? Are we only happy when well delineated, organized and scheduled actions take place, actions that can be recorded and advertised as such, or are we looking for a different kind of engagement, one that aims more toward unofficial, everyday encounters in the field that transform the dynamic of world making in local places and initiate action to the betterment of social conditions? This is, in the end, a question of who decides what is successful community engagement action, and on which grounds?

Finally, an important set of questions related to the success of any engagement project is that of the decisions taken during the process, and the impact these have on effective real, measurable change in a society. We believe that these questions are directly related to the quantified way that heritage management is perceived by large

DOI: 10.4324/9781003259367-6

organizations, research and teaching institutes. Part of an audit culture (Shore 2008, 279; Strathern 2000, 2) that seeks to measure and quantify social transformation and delineate change in demonstrable results that can be summarized in executive reports. This is part of what can be called a "state optic" (cf. Scott 1998) and we feel that it is as far from the experience of working with a community of people as can be conceived.

Why community engagement?

It is evident from what has been outlined in this book that we are talking from the prospect of archaeological and ethnographic 'experts' who seek to open up their research project to one or several communities of people directly related to it. So our version of setting up a collaborative project should take into account our position between the academic nexus, the state-managed archaeological landscape, local and national political institutions and the various groups and networks that crisscross the local landscape. This intermediary position makes the setting of clear goals a complicated exercise.

It is by now almost commonsensical for proponents of ethical practice in archaeology that the aim of engaged archaeology should be collaboration and inclusion in the published results (Colwell and Ferguson 2008; Atalay 2012, 43). While this is indeed a salutary and ethical aim for research projects, it sometimes achieves the opposite effect than the intended one: it embarks on a goal-setting exercise that does not reflect the desires and needs of local communities. On the contrary, it sets goals that are, at best, what the research project or institution *believes* that the locals want or should want. There are, however, cases such as the one described in this book, where the local community may not ultimately seek to be represented as an equal partner in scientific publications or presentation. For example, to mention the community, or specific names, as coauthors in a scientific article, may be a profoundly ethical act for archaeologists, and a stepping stone to persons within the community to a direct engagement with scientific archaeology or social science. However, the political economy of academic publications and the social capital associated with them are useful or interesting to the relatively enclosed field of academia. In our case at least, it has but limited impact in the livelihoods of locals. Conversely, local groups or individuals may demand that we invest time and resources from our research to produce content (written texts, exhibitions, public presentations, even entire museum collections) that has great significance and adds to social capital locally, but carries little, if any, weight in the academic field. This conundrum is inscribed in the realization of several ethnographers nowadays that a great part of social relations that are created in the field are impossible to include, in fact are inimical to academic publishing as it is (see e.g. Editorial Team 2013, 392).

In a similar fashion, while we may be willing to give up the privileges that our scientific 'expertise' gives us in favor of a more communal way of knowledge production, local and regional stakeholders may conversely *demand* that we strengthen and exercise this distinction in favor of local communities. Various examples we have presented in this book are emblematic of this conundrum that faces community projects in the field. The local communities and groups have very often asked us to become their cultural ambassadors of sorts, in their effort to combat marginalization in the new schemes for regional development and the envisioned increase in heritage and archaeological tourism in the area. Our intention to divest ourselves of all authority in meaning-making in the field thus collided with the political use that the local society wanted to make of our 'expertise'.

Who initiates a community project?

Our project was not one called for or prearranged by community members. It is clear that the decision to open the research process up and share it with local stakeholders was a decision mainly on the part of the original excavation team (Kyriakidis 2019). At any point during the process, the original initiative to do a public action was ours. But this often was confined to only initiating the action, making the first step to an avalanche of movements that led to the final result. For example, at the end of each public event, we held a communal meeting where the research process was discussed and we decided the next research theme. The decision was made together, and research was effectively steered by the participants toward what interests them most, rather than the other way around. When time came to put this planning to action, our role was that of the social animator and mediator, and sometimes the gadfly, to put the communal decision into practice. The question is therefore posed whether the institution, group or person who takes the initiative in such settings, who makes the first step, so to speak, essentially controls the whole process. This seemingly naïve question is, we think, what lies at the heart of the most radical definitions of community engagement. Colwell and Ferguson (2008), for example, posit the initiation of a project as one of the main characteristics that lead to community controlled projects.

However, it was one that was – one could say forcibly – appropriated by members of the local community to serve the village ends of development. From quite early on, the content of our research, our publications, our social media presence, was carefully screened by members of the community, and our ethnographic research was essentially directed to suit the capacities and desires of the village. Our approach and method seems to indicate, or take for granted, even, that community engagement is a good thing. Including the communities we work with in knowledge production not only makes for more sound ethical and counter-hegemonic practices, but also makes for better, richer, more relevant archaeology. The salutary effect of this approach for archaeology can scarcely be called in question, and indeed, numerous community-oriented projects around the world produce results that take the discipline forward both scientifically and in terms of positive impact for groups and communities. The process of archaeological ethnography, however, soon alerts us to a different angle to this question: do local communities want to be involved at all, and why would they want to get involved in the process of archaeological survey, excavation and exhibition. If they want to get involved, shouldn't the question be what they want to get involved in?

In our case, to put it simply, our interest in the Minoan past of the place was immense, but few individuals in the community shared the same intensity. Furthermore, their interest was not of the same kind and not fueled by the same background, ambitions and goals.

The expectations of engagement and different points of view

The open meeting is set for seven in the afternoon. The stones of the little square are still hot from the punishing sun, we are reaching the end of July and the usual temperate climate of the village has turned into full-blown summer. The doors of the surrounding houses are semi-open, to let the air in, but no activity can be discerned. We are waiting, in the small piazza at the far end of the village, for the villagers to come and discuss with us the future of the project. Nobody is here, besides the cidadas who are holding their deafening song. There are no chairs, no tables, nothing that makes this look remotely as a place of gathering. We look at each other in desperation, we take this as a sign that the villagers are not that interested in what we do. It is the first season of our summer school, and the students also look bewildered and weary. Just this morning, everybody sounded so eager and willing to help set up the meeting. The youngsters of the cultural association all agreed to bring chairs and tables, and to organize a little feast afterward. The punishing heat of the afternoon seems to have put everybody in a stupor. Nobody is picking up their mobile phones to our repetitive calls. We look at the screen once again: it is five to seven.

Just as our despair reaches its peak, a four wheel drive pickup truck arrives loaded to capacity with plastic chairs, stacked on piles that are held on their sides by young guys precariously balancing on the sides of the truck. The quiet square is now roaring with loud shouts, busy with people hurrying to and fro, carrying chairs, setting them up, all in a very relaxed and nonchalant, but still quick way. In the midst of all this, Mitsos stands shouting orders, cigarette in hand. To our protests, he responds with a convincing: "why do you feel stressed? We agreed, everything is going to be ready at seven." We soon understand that seven o'clock means different things to different people. By half past seven, the first villagers start to arrive, in an easy pace, like they are out on an afternoon stroll. Slowly, the village square begins to fill to capacity, and by half past eight almost everybody who is capable of coming is here. The meeting can begin.

This representative example of the way locals react to our efforts at community engagement is one of a series of incidents that have made us rethink what we mean by engagement. It especially made us rethink what we mean by engagement and whether our academically-gauged expectations of engagement and collaboration do in the end meet the desires, capacities and hopes of local communities we work with. When we arrive in the field, sometimes even after long stints of fieldwork, we still carry with us expectations and values of what constitutes successful engagement. Even the plainest of assumptions, such as the expectation of punctuality, of the character of verbal agreement and the level of obligation to the project, can very easily slip into colonial presumptions on our part. In practical terms, they draw from a hierarchy of values that gauges the level of interest expressed by the local community in our work, or their heritage. The levels of engagement can also be an indicator of indigenous resistance or refusal to cooperate.

In the past two decades especially, community engagement has become a buzzword for heritage practitioners. Every program or institution that needs to promote its social relevance feels obliged to have some sort of community activity on its list to show its compliance to an ethics of social inclusiveness. Community engagement has solidified in a series of activities and associated discourses that have only recently come under critical scrutiny. Most of the criticisms addressed toward community engagement practices focus on the assumed notion of community itself. As Steve Watson and Emma Waterton aptly put it, community engagement has "been encouraged by the box ticking expediencies associated with ideas about social inclusiveness, especially where these were the product of political imperatives that celebrated the value of community without ever examining its definition or content." (Watson and Waterton 2010, 1).

The problem with such approaches is that they content that a community is already somehow there, waiting for the researcher or practitioner to arrive and engage it. In an earlier chapter of this book, we have highlighted some of the issues involved in locating and identifying the local community, especially in the light of somewhat recent processes of dispersal, and the advent of social media and other forms of communication. In other parts, we have described the many different groups and networks that exist in a placed community, and their often conflicting values, motives and expectations. From our years of working in and with the people of Gonies, we have realized that speaking about "the local community" is nothing more than a useful catch-all phrase. Although it is handy to communicate with, it is not an adequately descriptive sociological term. On the other hand, however, there is indeed this sense of "being in place" that some locals have a name for (i.e. "Gonianosyni"), and it helps these wild agglomerates of people stay in place, it adds resilience, it fosters hope and very real networks of support and communication.

We would therefore have to circumvent the issues presented in community engagement by stating a rather obvious fact, that remains unsaid: that different community-focused activities will engage various audiences and groups within the sum of people that inhabit or are related to a place. We could therefore claim, to take it one step further, that engagement is the action that *creates* communities of interest, rather than the other way around. To make this more specific, the level of analysis for the whole community is not the same as that for the communities that are created through activities of engagement. And although we try to include the entirety of people in a community, there are few ways to do that with a single activity or project. Different projects will engage and speak differently to different people within the same group.

As we have already discussed before, this simple fact makes it even more necessary, even ethically imperative, to make ethnographic research a constituent element of all such efforts at engagement. Embedded research can alert us to the differences within a social group we may initially understand as unstratified, undifferentiated and whole, and therefore direct our collaborative activities in tune with the needs and desires of persons, groups and stakeholders. We hope that it is clear from what has preceded this chapter that community engagement is not and cannot be a set of centrally planned activities that are executed in a one-off fashion. On the contrary, it is a long-term process, that involves constant research in the field, constant interaction to achieve collaborative design, and a long, sometimes tortuous, reflexive period in preparation for the next step.

Collaborative work to what end?

The second important issue, demonstrated in the example we opened this chapter with, is the definition of engagement. Not so much in a theoretical sense, whereby it is classified in easily assessed categories, but in terms of practice. Several decades onwards from the social justice movements of the 1960s and 1970s through which indigenous movements sought and gained greater control over archaeological research, the question of collaboration or engagement in archaeological and heritage research still remains open and fluid (Zimmermann 2006, 39). The goal of most collaborative work is to redress the perceived imbalance between researcher and subject community by establishing equality in all stages of the research process: planning, funding, executing and managing the impact (Colwell and Ferguson 2008). Working definitions of engagement or collaboration are sufficiently vague to allow projects themselves to define their activities in the ways that are most suitable for them (La Salle 2010, 406).

From our experience, engagement reflects an affective economy of attention that balances the expectations of researchers and heritage managers with the goals, resources and habits of groups of people. This means first of all that collaboration has a different content for engaged communities and for research teams. Both parties expect different things, can invest different resources, and have different capacities. But secondly, that the success of a collaboration must be judged in terms of the local context, and not in terms of deterritorialized academic discourse.

The main issue that we see here, which is frequently overlooked in discussions of unequal distribution of power, is not the knowledge gap, but something altogether different: to be an 'expert' means that you are somehow paid to devote the majority of your time to a specific task, in this case heritage preservation and management. But the communities you are working with do not have this luxury: what they offer is not only their knowledge, resources, or interest, but also, and perhaps more importantly, their spare time. Time they may or may not have outside the time they spend to earn a living. In the context of the so-called Greek crisis, this surplus time became even more precious, as many people were pressed to find a second job, or engage in other forms of subsistence making, such as small-scale agriculture or animal husbandry. The people who we expect to come to our meetings, our events, or the very people we expect to be available for interviews, discussions or other forms of ethnographic engagement are actually volunteering their time, which in the context of late capitalism has become a significant resource.

So we would like to take a step back from discussions of uneven distribution of power, that are usually based on the control of discourses and content, to look at the essence of engagement, which is the occupation of shared time and space. Without it, engagement does not happen. This shared time and space becomes a node for a series of political economic flows, presided in our case by the attention economy that the neoliberal university wants to command. Most community projects begin with the unquestioned assumption that the communities addressed share, or should share, the same interest in their heritage that 'experts' do. The base assumption is that communities of people understand and feel that local heritage is of utmost importance, and occupies a large part of their daily life and identity formation. But this link of identity formation and everyday livelihood is not clear in practice, and may be altogether absent. The performative time of heritage is often very much different than what occupies the day of most people in the field. So when we ask them to put it center stage, we are actually asking them to change the ways they make a living and take a step outside their everyday lives that has immediate material repercussions on their lives. In the example we presented above, the people who volunteered to help us in setting up the village meeting were working most of the day, and had but little time to go back home, get some rest and get up again to get on phones and knock on doors to muster everybody else, probably also asleep after an exhausting day at work.

We often asked ourselves in the field, why do they do it? Why volunteer this time and effort to create these cultural events in the village? We gradually realized that the affective side of this gathering of resources, people and interest was more important than its material side. And this, in our view gauged the success of the project in ways that are important and impactful to the people themselves, albeit not perhaps to the concerned institutions – universities, funding bodies and municipal authorities. This is the other important issue that remains undiscussed in much of the literature: the very process that pronounces a project successful still remains outside the control of local communities. And this judgement is never made on the terms of the community itself. The affective weight, or the existential support rendered by engaged projects in the field is never gauged in reports or performance reviews.

Decision-making and the political uses of 'experts'

The other issue we need to address is the scope of decision-making in community controlled heritage projects (e.g. Colwell-Chantaphonh and Ferguson 2007). If we look at scientific or other projects that have been invited by a local place, we need to ask who exactly made this decision. Was it tribal elders or persons with political power or prestige in the community? Was it some sort of democratic decision-making body? Was it a local authority? In our experience, when a project is initiated locally, it means that a few people made a decision and pushed it forward, with a level of tacit acceptance from the other members of a community, rather than a wholehearted endorsement by them. The municipality-funded excavations already mentioned in earlier chapters, as well as others currently active in different parts of Crete (e.g. on the Plateau of Lasithi) could nominally be seen as community-driven projects. However, when examined closely, the political decision to initiate and fund an excavation, for example, does not imply direct involvement of a community. In fact, in several cases, these projects are conducted without effective public involvement. This is, we feel, indicative not only of the lack of planning for community engagement, but also a symptom of broader social and political processes. The political function of communities as decision-making bodies, especially rural ones, has been replaced in the past few decades with token representatives that have little or no real power to decide the future of the place in local or regional bodies. As we analyze in greater detail in (Anagnostopoulos and Kyriakidis, forthcoming), this creates a context where the collaboration with local stakeholders has to be carefully created from scratch. Instead of arriving in the field with a preconceived notion of communal decision-making, with a naive version of the community as an unproblematic common, and with a tokenist approach to political personnel as representatives of a community, we have instead been faced with the challenge to set up decision-making bodies focused on minor but crucial decisions on the content and outreach of heritage projects.

With the above we do not claim that locals are powerless or operate outside networks of power that have translocal reach. What we argue is that there is no institution, or process, or relevant custom that may enable such communities to reach inclusive decisions on the management of their own heritage. In the absence of established processes of decision-making that concern even small parts of their communal life and future, this lack is part of the bigger picture of communities in Greece in the present. Simultaneously, the limited space that the Greek state allows local societies to decide about the management of their own heritage (Voudouri 2010, 555) reflects the disbelief with which it approaches communities as stakeholders, stewards, or owners of such heritage, and is probably the main reason why this is an area of conflict rather than agreement (Herzfeld 1991, 34). As some have indicated, the top-down, authoritarian approach of the Greek state is detrimental to any active involvement by 'non-experts' (Fouseki 2009).

Sometimes, the assumption that the researcher is with the side of power and privilege does not help the project team identify the real power struggles within a community and the ability of groups and persons to divert and employ the project's status for their own ends, that are unclear to the uninitiated eye.

In 2012, we were called to participate in a meeting of all the cultural associations from villages in the area. A well-known photographer who is a descendant of a well-known Goniote family had proposed an idea for a torch-lit process from nearby villages to the top of Philioremos, a performative event that he was positive would attract hundreds of visitors and audiences world-wide. We arrived at the only kafeneio in the center of Kamariotis, a near-deserted historic village not far from Gonies, on the western edge of the small plateau right below the village. As it was getting darker, we were greeted by two elderly inhabitants and the shop owner, and walked in the kafeneio that also serves as a sort of local museum. Under the framed vests of local warlords from nineteenth century insurrections against Ottoman rule, the representatives from cultural associations started gathering slowly. As one by one walked in the shop, we began to realize that relationships between them were cordial only on the surface. The pleasantries and salutations exchanged showed a deep-seated mistrust and reserve, despite the friendly personal relationships between some of them. Our position in the discussion became gradually more awkward, as we began to ponder why exactly we were called in the meeting. It was certainly a decision of the Goniote part, that aimed to ensure that the proposition that this photographer made had some sort of "scientific" basis, even when this meant the approval of an archaeological team. At the same time, however, our presence there also strengthened the

Goniote position in the discussion: they were the ones with the 'experts' on their side. Our presence weighed down on the meeting without us being aware that it did. While, therefore, at first we were exhilarated with our ability to mediate between cultural associations in the area, as we reflected further on the event, it transpired to us that our presence may have actually deepened the rift between the associations as we may have unwittingly played heavily on the Goniote side. In a fiercely egalitarian society, where braggers or show-offs are quickly taken down in public or are made the butt of gossip and jokes, the Goniote audacity at arriving full-force at the meeting was taken in by a very large degree of mistrust and reluctance. This was made very plain in the meeting itself, as well as the communications between members and officials in the associations later on. All the associations from neighboring villages were concerned that this was a move by Gonies to exert their hegemony over the area. The refusal to cooperate was based on the explicit concern that this was all a Goniote ploy to use people and resources from other villages to bring visitors to their village, and show that their cultural landmarks were the most important in the area.

This example shows how we begin our work with the best intentions and may assume our role as cultural mediators, without being aware of the power struggles inherent in a specific setting, that may have, and usually do have, very deep historical roots, unseen at first.

But it is also to do with something more important: that our theoretical alertness at seeing colonial and hegemonic tendencies at work in academic research does not make us equally ready to accept that we may enter networks of power that we have no control over. This is a double-pronged move, that may ironically perpetuate the degradation of locals by both overestimating the powers of knowledge from the academic side, and underestimating locals as powerless individuals.

It has been our contention throughout this book that ethnographic research further highlights the vicissitudes of taking for granted apparently communal decisions on heritage management as unanimous and wholehearted. As an embedded method of research and action, it brings to the fore the myriad strategies, political tensions and clashes between individuals and groups that may not be visible to the practitioner who does not take the time to pore over them.

References

Anagnostopoulos, Aris and Evangelos Kyriakidis. 2022. "From Community Archaeology to Heritage Making: Ethnographic Observations on Building

Collaborative Processes through Archaeological Projects." In: Lena Stefanou and Ioanna Antoniadou (eds.), *Journal of Community Archaeology and Heritage*, special issue.

Atalay, Sonia. 2012. *Community-Based Archaeology: Research with, by, and for Indigenous and Local Communities*. Berkeley, CA: University of California Press.

Colwell-Chanthaphonh, Chip, and Thomas Ferguson. 2008. "Introduction: The Collaborative Continuum." In: Chip Colwell-Chanthaphonh and Thomas Ferguson (eds.) *Collaboration in Archaeological Practice: Engaging Descendant Communities*. Lanham, MD: AltaMira Press.

Editorial Team. 2013. "Public Ethnography: An Introduction to the Special Issue." *Qualitative Research* 13 (4): 391–401.

Fouseki, Kalliopi. 2009. "'I Own, therefore I Am': Conflating Archaeology with Heritage in Greece: A Possessive Individualist Approach." In: Emma Waterton and Laurajane Smith (eds.), *Taking Archaeology Out of Heritage*. Cambridge: Cambridge Scholars Publishing, 49–65.

Herzfeld, Michael. 1991. *A Place in History: Social and Monumental Time in a Cretan Town*. Princeton, NJ: Princeton University Press.

Kyriakidis, Evangelos, 2019. *A Community Empowerment Approach to Heritage Management: From Values Assessment to Local Engagement*. London: Routledge.

La Salle, Marina. 2010. "Community Collaboration and Other Good Intentions." *Archaeologies: Journal of the World Archaeological Congress* 6 (3): 401–22.

Scott, James C. 1998. *Seeing Like a State: How Certain Schemes to Improve the Human Condition have Failed*. New Haven, CT: Yale University Press.

Shore, Chris. 2008. "Audit Culture and Illiberal Governance: Universities and the Politics of Accountability." *Anthropological Theory* 8 (3): 278–98.

Strathern, Marilyn. 2000. "Introduction: New Accountabilities. Anthropological Studies in Audit, Ethics and the Academy." In: Marilyn Strathern (ed.), *Audit Cultures. Anthropological Studies in Accountability, Ethics and the Academy*. London: Routledge.

Voudouri, Dafni. 2010. "Law and the Politics of the Past: Legal Protection of Cultural Heritage in Greece." *International Journal of Cultural Property* 17 (3): 547–68.

Watson, Steve and Emma Waterton. 2010. "Introduction: Heritage and Community Engagement - Finding a New Agenda." In: Emma Waterton and Steve Watson (eds.), *Heritage and Community Engagement: Collaboration or Contestation?* London: Routledge.

Zimmerman, Larry. 2006. "Consulting Stakeholders." In: Jane Balme and Alistair Paterson (eds.), *Archaeology in Practice: A Student Guide to Archaeological Analyses*. London: Blackwell, 39–58.

Index

128   *Index*